Playing the Game While Black Womaning in Corporate America™

Your ultimate playbook in navigating power, perception, and prejudice in the workplace

By Nicole S. Palmer

Published by Delnic Media LLC

Dedication

To every Black queen who has ever felt unseen, underestimated, or held back by the unspoken rules. This book is for you — to remind you of your power, your resilience, and your undeniable place in every room you step into. May you always navigate with purpose, dignity, and fierce determination within you.

Acknowledgments

To my rock, my unwavering foundation: Thank you for being my constant compass and anchor through this journey's highs and lows. Even when I doubted myself, your belief in me has been a guiding light. This book would have been impossible without your steadfast support, patience, and love. You reminded me that my voice matters, that my story deserves to be told, and that I have the strength to see this through.

To my mentors and confidants: Thank you for your insights, encouragement, and unfiltered advice. Whether you knew it or not, each of you helped shape the perspectives in this book. You taught me how to navigate challenges with resilience, to see through the noise, and always to hold my ground. From those long talks to the subtle nudges that pushed me forward, your guidance has been a lifeline in this journey.

To the sisterhood of Black women in corporate America: This book is as much about your strength as it is a guide. You've reminded me that I am not alone in this game through shared stories, silent nods, and unspoken understandings. Your brilliance and unwavering solidarity have inspired these pages and provided the support to keep pushing forward. This is for us, every room we enter, and the legacy we're building together.

I extend my deepest gratitude to Barry Beckham, "jefe," for giving me my start as an intern in the early 2000s. Barry, thank you for your guidance and support and for taking the time to review my initial book proposal. I will never forget your words, "This is going to be bigger than you realize." That simple yet powerful affirmation gave me the confidence to leap forward, to believe in this work, and to bring this vision to life. I look forward to you saying, "I told you so," when this takes off.

Last but certainly not least, to my mom, AKA Queen Esther... thank you for constantly pushing me and always believing I could do anything I set my mind to. Thank you for being part of the cheering squad when I wasn't entirely sure if I dared to bring this book to life.

Table of Contents

Preface

I was sixteen when I packed my bags and left for college with a full-tuition scholarship to a private school in the DMV. Tuition was covered, but everything else — books, room, food, life — wasn't. I needed a job. Fast.

Thankfully, our dorm was right next to a hospital. I applied for a role in admissions and soon found myself registering patients for procedures and hospital stays. It wasn't glamorous, but it paid the bills, and the hospital's round-the-clock schedule allowed me to work around my classes. Most weeks, I clocked forty hours while juggling a full course load. It was a grind, but it worked.

That job became more than just a paycheck. It was a lifeline — and my first real taste of leadership. At seventeen, I was promoted to team lead, a position I knew I was the most qualified for, even if I wasn't everyone's favorite pick. That role taught me the value of showing up, doing the work, and proving your worth, even when the odds are stacked against you.

But the hospital job gave me more than leadership experience — it lit a spark in me. I saw how systems worked behind the scenes to connect patients to care and how much effort it took to ensure things ran smoothly. For the first time, I began thinking about how health and access intersect, and that curiosity grew into a passion. That job set me on the path to pursuing a public health education, even if I didn't fully realize it then.

Stepping into leadership gave me a confidence boost, which I carried with me when I decided to venture into the "real" world. At nineteen, I took on a department head position at a small, scrappy company. It sounded like a dream, but the reality hit hard. I quickly learned that a big title came with even bigger expectations — and no real support. Burnout set in fast, and I realized I wasn't ready for the relentless demands or the politics of corporate America.

That experience taught me a harsh but necessary lesson: not all workplaces are created equal, and not all leadership roles are worth the cost. After that, I gravitated back to the hospital for a decade since I remained on the payroll as a part-timer. It was my safety net.

My supervisor there — a mentor who saw my potential when others didn't — always kept her word: "You'll always have a job here." She created a bubble where my work spoke for itself, my contributions were valued, and I had room to grow. Her belief in me gave me the courage to take risks, knowing I had a soft place to land.

When she passed away, that bubble burst. The protective shield I'd relied on, and the safety net she had built for me was gone. While the hospital still offered opportunities, it wasn't the same without her leadership and guidance. I found myself at a crossroads — staying in a familiar environment that had become bittersweet or pushing myself into uncharted territory to discover my capabilities. I chose the latter, even though it meant stepping into the unknown.

Stepping into the unknown looked like taking on temp stints at various companies to pay the bills and determine my next steps. I worked in roles that ranged from proofreader to assistant editor, picking up skills and insights into how different workplaces operated. Temping gave me a front-row seat to office dynamics without pulling me into the thick of the bureaucracy. I observed how influence flowed, decisions were made, and relationships shaped the culture, but I didn't yet have the context to understand what I was seeing fully.

My last temp stint changed everything. It evolved into a permanent position, and the pieces started to fall into place. With a permanent role came more responsibility, higher stakes, and a closer view of the unspoken rules that governed success — or failure. Suddenly, I realized that this wasn't just about doing the work but navigating the game. The workplace wasn't a meritocracy; it was a chessboard. And while I didn't know all the moves yet, I started paying attention, one observation at a time.

This book is my way of sharing what I've learned. I'm framing corporate life as a game of chess — not to intimidate, but to help you make sense of the moves. You don't need to know how to play chess to get this. All you need is the determination to define success on your terms.

For every Black woman navigating corporate America, this is your playbook. The game may be rigged, but I hope that understanding the rules and how to play them to your advantage allows you to embrace and amplify the power already within you.

Introduction

Welcome. If you're holding this book, you likely already realize that corporate America isn't just about "do good work, get rewarded." For us, it's more like a slow-burn game of chess, requiring strategy, patience, and the ability to anticipate others' moves.

As the first book in this series, *Playing the Game While Black Womaning in Corporate America*™ lays the foundation for understanding corporate life's complexities and unspoken rules, especially for Black women. This journey begins here, but each book in the series will delve deeper into the different facets of "the game."

The game involves understanding the board and the unspoken dynamics for Black women. But we don't come to it empty-handed. We bring grit, insight, and a unique perspective built through our experiences. No strategy can replicate that.

In chess, each piece holds a unique power—a role that contributes to the whole and shapes the board. As you move through this book, you'll see these pieces come to life as roles within corporate America and as representations of the internal assets you bring to the game. The king, for instance, is the gatekeeper, someone whose influence controls access to vital opportunities. But the king also represents something more personal: your reputation. Once fortified, it's a cornerstone asset that defines and protects your career trajectory.

This duality is intentional and essential. In every corporate setting, you navigate two landscapes: the external players and the internal assets you protect. It means recognizing that the queen isn't just the high-ranking Black woman whose example might inspire you. She also represents your unique talents, strengths, and values — the crown that defines you.

Each chapter will give you strategies to protect your assets and skillfully navigate the players who shape your journey. This book is designed to help you see these dualities clearly, equipping you to make calculated moves while staying true to yourself.

This book breaks down these insights into ten distinct chapters. Each builds on the last to take you from understanding the basics of "the game" to making masterful moves that balance success with self-preservation.

Here's what you can expect in each chapter:

- **Chapter 1: Read the Rules**—Discover the seven universal rules that govern corporate America for Black women, laying a foundation for every chapter that follows.
- **Chapter 2: Learn the Participants**—Identify key "pieces" on the corporate board, from allies to opponents, and understand how they influence your career journey.
- **Chapter 3: Study the Board**—Observe and decode the organizational structure, power dynamics, and hidden currents influencing your workplace.
- **Chapter 4: Guard Your Crown**—Prioritize protecting your unique strengths, talents, and mental well-being—your "crown"—against

the pressures and biases of corporate spaces.

- **Chapter 5: Protect Your Rep** — Preserve and defend your professional reputation, "the king," safeguarding this critical asset from potential damage.
- **Chapter 6: Take Center Stage** — Position yourself visibly and strategically, ensuring your contributions and presence are recognized without risking overexposure.
- **Chapter 7: Think Ten Steps Ahead** — Anticipate challenges and seize opportunities through proactive, forward-thinking career planning.
- **Chapter 8: Know Your Opponents** — Identify workplace antagonists who may obstruct your progress and employ strategies to navigate adversarial dynamics.
- **Chapter 9: Build Your Defense** — Strengthen your position with strategies for self-protection in corporate settings, from setting boundaries to documenting contributions.

- **Chapter 10: Check, Not Mate** — Master strategic restraint, choosing when to engage and when to hold back with purpose and intention.

While each chapter generally follows a consistent structure, certain elements vary to best address the unique challenges covered. Here's what you can expect in most chapters:

- **Key Sections**: Each chapter is divided into manageable sections that tackle unique challenges Black women face, offering context, insights, and strategies for navigating them.
- **Strategy for Success**: At the end of most sections, you'll find a "**Strategy for Success**" — an actionable takeaway you can use immediately.
- **Rule Insights**: Concepts within each chapter frequently tie back to the seven rules from Chapter One, serving as a connecting thread throughout the book.

- **Key Takeaways**: Each chapter often concludes with a concise summary that distills the main points and emphasizes practical lessons. These takeaways ensure that, even after you close the chapter, you're equipped with clear and memorable steps to apply in your journey.
- **Food for Thought:** Most chapters close with reflective prompts encouraging deeper self-exploration. These questions and challenges are an invitation to connect the chapter's themes to your own experiences, fostering personal growth and insight, and the chance to define how you'll bring these lessons into your career and life.

This book is both a guide and a companion — it is not about "leaning in" or cracking codes but about making intentional moves that preserve your peace, power, and pride. So, let's dive in and approach this game with strategy, strength, and a mindset that keeps you in control.

Chapter 1: Read the Rules

Welcome to the Game Board

When it comes to corporate America—which I'll more often than not refer to as "the board" from now on—I tasted its harsh reality in increments. My early days were spent in the safety net of a hospital job, shielded by a leader and mentor who valued my abilities and ensured I had room to grow. From there, I bounced between temp assignments and roles that lasted for one- to three-year stretches. I became a department head at much too young an age at a company that operated on fumes and coffee, where I got my first dose of corporate culture—a brutal crash course in grit, sacrifice, and survival. My days started long before the sun, often stretching late into the night with little more than scotch tape and bubble gum to hold things together.

After I moved on from there, temp assignments exposed me to a mix of workplaces, each with its quirks and unwritten rules. But it wasn't until I landed what I'd call my first substantive corporate role that I came face-to-face with the actual game, the one that would later define my understanding of the board. Here, I learned the hard truth: this game wasn't designed for someone like me. It was rigged and could drain you if you let it.

When I started this job, I expected long hours, a steep learning curve, and maybe even some politics. But nothing prepared me for the complexity of unspoken rules and the mental tightrope I'd be walking. That job left a lasting mark — physically, mentally, spiritually, and emotionally. I'd entered with the drive to succeed and prove myself, but I quickly learned that success here meant learning to play a game I didn't even know I'd signed up for.

Here's what I learned: the game isn't fair. It never will be. But knowing the rules can make all the difference. Pay attention to how decisions are made, who holds the real power, and how influence flows in your workplace. It's not just about working hard; it's about working smart, which starts with understanding the game.

This book is my way of pulling back the curtain on that game. The rules I outline here weren't passed down in any training manual. They're hard-earned lessons from years of navigating a world that wasn't set up for me—or, frankly, people like me: Black women as a whole. As you move through each chapter, you'll see the threads of these experiences woven throughout, each a reminder of the tactics it takes to play in a system that often feels like it's actively working against you.

But first things first: the rules.

Rule 1: Nobody talks about playing the game.

Think of this first rule as the corporate world's version of *Fight Club*. The unspoken agreement is explicit: don't talk about the game—not with colleagues, friends, or even yourself in moments of frustration. The first time I realized this rule was fundamental, I was years into that corporate role—the one that would ultimately test every assumption I had about hard work, talent, and success.

When I first entered that office, I came in armed with my skills, drive, and the belief that if I worked hard and showed up, my contributions would speak for themselves. But corporate America isn't a meritocracy; it's a game played in hushed tones, back channels, and invisible alliances. The entire system is designed to keep the rules just out of sight.

Yet the game was everywhere: in the structure of meetings, in the subtle phrasing of emails, and, perhaps most insidiously, in the spaces where I wasn't invited. At first, I thought it was just me overthinking things, chalking it up to "impostor syndrome." But then, time and again, I'd see the same people rewarded, the same voices amplified, while others, voices that looked and sounded like mine, were notably absent. And when I tried to bring it up, I'd get the same response: silence or a good old-fashioned brushoff.

Recognizing the Hidden Rules

The first part of mastering this rule is recognizing that it exists. If you're new to the board, the rules won't be handed to you on a silver platter. For most of us, they'll become apparent only after a series of setbacks or observations. In those early years, I learned one painful truth: my drive and ambition were only pieces on the board, tools to be used in a game that, I would later realize, I was often invited to only in service of someone else's end.

The first clue came when I was excluded from a major project I had been initially asked to lead. I'd put in countless weeks putting the project together, only to find out that I wasn't going to get to present the project. I learned about this haphazardly the day the project was to be presented to the higher-ups. I was asked to provide cliff notes to the presenter. The critical difference between us, other than the fact that one of us was the subject-matter expert and the other wasn't — was that the person didn't look like me.

Talking About the Game Will Cost You

The second part of this rule is understanding the consequences of ignoring it. In corporate America, calling out the game is often seen as a threat. If you're the one who dares to ask, "Why did this person get the project?" or "How are decisions being made here?" you've branded yourself as a problem. And problems in corporate settings are often handled — not solved.

The few times I tried to question the structure and why certain people were always in the room and others were not, I quickly saw the cost. My questions were met with polite smiles, vague reassurances, or silence. I'd find myself mysteriously left out of future projects or critical meetings, with opportunities subtly slipping through my fingers. I was learning the hard way that nobody calls out the lopsidedness of the game out loud (i.e., in mixed company or unsafe spaces). Those who do often find themselves on the outside looking in.

Finding Allies on the Board

Over time, I realized that while nobody talks about the game, some see it as clearly as you do. They may not say it outright, but they'll catch your eye in a meeting when someone's been particularly overbearing or offer a quiet "I noticed that, too" when things don't add up. These are the silent observers who play along but keep their own counsel. They know the stakes, but they also understand the importance of survival.

Finding allies in corporate spaces isn't easy. They're rarely the loudest voices or the ones dominating the spotlight. They're often the individuals who keep their heads down but whose words carry weight when they choose to speak. When you find one of these quiet observers, cultivate that relationship. They're often the ones who can give you insights into the game if you're trying to find your footing.

Playing Without Saying a Word

Mastering Rule 1 isn't about remaining silent forever, it's about learning to play the game without needing to name it. To excel on the board as a Black woman means adopting strategies that allow you to navigate spaces, gain influence, and build your career while maintaining the silent code. You can call out bias, push for recognition, and advocate for yourself without ever uttering the phrase, "This game is rigged."

The trick is to become fluent in the language of subtlety, learn how to advocate without alienating and stand out without stepping on toes. That might mean strategically positioning yourself in meetings, finding ways to elevate your visibility without relying on formal structures, or learning to make your voice heard authentically and effectively.

The power in playing this game isn't in saying what it is. It's in knowing exactly how to navigate it without needing to state the obvious.

Breaking the Silence for Future Players

But while we're here, let me say this: we can — and should — change up the game's rules, even if we play by them now. One of the most powerful things we can do is reach back, pull another Black woman aside, and share what we've learned. Imagine if, from day one, every Black woman in corporate America had someone who took her aside and explained the unspoken rules. Imagine if none of us had to waste years figuring out the game on our own.

These days, I see younger generations entering corporate spaces with a fire in their hearts and a refusal to accept what they've been handed. And let me tell you, that fire makes me so proud. It's powerful and necessary to question the status quo, push back against injustice, and demand change. These young people are standing up and declaring that they're done with business as usual — and that's something I wish more of us could have done openly years ago.

But here's where the mother hen in me steps in. With all that righteous energy and boldness comes a caution: as Black women, the game isn't fair, and the rules aren't the same. Corporate America wasn't built with us in mind, and sometimes, pushing back too hard or fast can have repercussions that hit us differently than they might for others. Experience teaches us that microaggressions and blatant biases aren't just frustrating — they're part of a system that has real power to set us back if we're not careful.

I've been on the receiving end of more retaliatory actions and behaviors than I care to recount merely because I was direct, open, and honest: three things that label any competent and intelligent Black woman as a threat. Suddenly, you're no longer the go-to or the "rock star" you were dubbed at the outset. Now you're angry. Difficult. Not a team player. That is the danger of speaking truth to power when the power in question has absolutely no interest in hearing what you have to say.

I don't say this to diminish anyone's spirit or to sound like the auntie who's always telling you to "be careful." This is about learning to navigate without losing that fire. I've been around long enough to have seen what happens when we go in with our heads held high but our shields down. The backlash can be swift, and our stakes are often much higher. I hope to offer the perspective that while we push for change, we also pace ourselves and stay vigilant, protecting our essence while demanding our place at the table. Or as is the case for many high-performing, high-achieving Black women, build your own table.

This isn't a call to broadcast strategies on every conference call. It's about creating safe spaces where we can talk openly and freely, share the lessons without fear, and remind each other that while we may have to follow Rule 1 in the boardroom, we can rewrite it together. It's a behind-the-scenes revolution, one conversation at a time.

Sometimes, the most extraordinary power comes not from playing the game in silence but from finding moments to speak about it, one sister to another. While Rule 1 may keep us safe today, breaking it—together—will make us powerful tomorrow.

Rule 2: There Are No Spectators

On the board, "just doing your job" isn't a shield; it's a move. Whether you know it or not, you've been a participant since day one. There's no safe distance where you can sit back and stay above the fray and no invisibility cloak that lets you slip under the radar. Even staying quiet, keeping your head down, and steering clear of office politics—none of it exempts you from the game. You're still in it, whether you're strategizing at the table or waiting for cues from others.

I learned this the hard way. Fresh in a role, I thought staying out of the mix would protect me from the undercurrents of corporate politics. I clocked in, hit my goals, and stayed focused on the work itself, thinking results would speak louder than whatever politics played out around me. But I quickly learned that silence on the board isn't neutral—it's a statement, often one that others will define for you.

Before I fully understood how the game operated, I'd get comments from colleagues like, "You know, I thought you were really stuck-up until I got to know you!" At first, I let it roll off with a laugh, but it happened so often that I realized these labels had a life of their own. They weren't based on my work or my inter-actions; they were projections — labels as-signed to me because I kept to myself. I wasn't socializing or going out of my way to make friends. And, in a world that rewards the familiar, my decision to stay in my lane made me "stuck up" or "cold." For a lot of Black women, this is a harsh reality: people will fill in your si-lence with whatever story suits them best. And once the label sticks, peeling it off can take years.

This experience taps into what scholars term hypervisibility. In corporate spaces, Black women are often hypervisible, standing out in ways we don't control while still being perceived as outsiders. Our presence in a meeting or silence at a lunch isn't just a non-event; it's noticed, analyzed, and, more often than not, as-signed meaning we never intended. Hy-pervisibility means that even our quiet moments carry a weight, a symbolism others impose on us, often without understanding who we are or why we choose not to engage. And if hypervisibility is the reality, then so is the double-edged sword of every action being visible and misunderstood.

How the Board Defines the "Quiet" Players

Here's the hidden part of Rule 2: the corporate game has no seats for spectators but plenty of labels for those who sit on the sidelines. If you choose to be quiet and do only what's asked of you, understand that this game is ready to brand you with whatever title best suits its needs. "Reliable but lacking initiative," "competent but invisible," or the classic "good enough." Corporate spaces love labels for the ones who aren't actively in the mix.

Being a "quiet" player doesn't mean you're left out of the game. It means you're giving others the space to define your role, your worth, and your place on the board. And more often than not, those labels stick. The corporate world thrives on narratives; if you're not shaping yours, someone else will.

Moves That Go Unseen — Until They Don't

The irony of Rule 2 is that even the most subtle moves are noticed in corporate spaces. Who you talk to, the meetings you prioritize, and the times you choose not to speak up — all these actions and non-actions tell a story. And in a space where everyone competes for visibility, silence can be its own form of standout behavior. I remember skipping a team-building lunch, not because I wasn't interested, but because I had pressing deadlines. But that absence was noted. Colleagues started to joke, "Oh, she's all work and no play," and it stuck longer than I would have liked. Suddenly, I was "the serious one," a label that defined my role within my team.

In the board, if you're not in control of your story, you're leaving it open for interpretation — and interpretations here tend to align with the storyteller's interests, not yours. Even silence has a way of speaking loudly in these spaces, and without your input, the volume can be cranked up to say things you never intended.

You're Either Gaining Ground or Losing It

You're constantly moving toward influence or away from it on the board. Playing it safe may feel comfortable, but safety here is a mirage. The unspoken truth of Rule 2 is that every inch you refuse to take is ground given to someone else. And in a world where resources, opportunities, and recognition are limited, you can't afford to lose ground.

If you're not actively seeking to expand your reach, someone else is. And they'll use that ground to frame the story of who you are, your potential, and what you bring to the table. Every meeting you skip, every comment you hold back, every chance to connect you let pass— they're not just missed opportunities. They're moves in the game that create space for others to advance.

The Power of Playing While "Quiet"

But let's be clear: This isn't a call to become a loud, relentless player who fights for every scrap of visibility. There's a strategy for maintaining a measured silence and speaking only when your words carry weight. If you prefer to play quietly, know that this, too, is a form of influence, it just requires precision.

Playing the game quietly but powerfully means choosing when and where you make your moves. It's about observing who holds sway, who respects your contributions, and where you can carve out a place to influence without sacrificing your principles. It might mean positioning yourself in less conventional ways but allowing your voice to be heard when it matters. Quiet players aren't invisible; they're strategic. They choose their moves carefully, ensuring that it counts when they speak or act.

In corporate spaces, silence isn't a lack of participation, it's a position. And if you're choosing to be a quiet player, make sure your silence isn't passive. It should be a silence that observes, absorbs, and calculates. Make it intentional, grounded in an awareness of how every move — or non-move — shapes the game around you.

Rule 3: Their best is your mediocre.

On the board, there's a set of unspoken expectations for Black women that often contradict the standards applied to everyone else. Your best won't be seen as excellent, it'll be seen as the baseline, the bare minimum to stay in the game. You might find yourself working twice as hard yet told you're barely meeting expectations. It's a reality that can drain you if you're unprepared, but understanding this rule is the first step in navigating it without losing yourself.

Early on, I remember being part of a team project that required a last-minute overhaul. Deadlines were tight, and the stakes were high. I stayed late, reworking the presentation, combing through data, and refining every line until it was seamless. When I presented it, I'd poured hours into perfecting every detail. The response? A polite nod, a brief "thank you," and then the team lead quickly moved on. Later, I overheard that same lead praising another team member's contribution — work I'd had to redo in the final hour. And it hit me: the standards were different. For some, showing up was enough to earn applause; for me, excellence was merely expected, barely worth acknowledging.

Why the Bar is Higher

This is the reality of Rule 3. For Black women, competence isn't a badge of honor; it's the price of entry. You're expected to bring your A-game but don't expect the same accolades or recognition that others get for less. When you perform well, it's simply what's expected; when others do, it's celebrated as brilliance. It's an experience that countless Black women have encountered, navigating spaces where their efforts are rendered invisible even as they shoulder more of the weight.

Understanding this dynamic is essential because it's not about lowering your standards or downplaying your achievements, it's about recalibrating your expectations. The praise you might hope for may never come, but that doesn't mean your work goes unnoticed. Every polished report, flawless presentation, and project delivered on time builds your credibility, even if the applause is sparse.

Navigating The Double Standards on the Board

What nobody tells you is how deeply entrenched these double standards are. When others slip up, it's "a learning experience." When you slip up, it's a mark against your competency. When others show up unprepared, it's overlooked. When you show up ready but stumble on a single point, it's scrutinized.

There was a time when I had to present a proposal to an executive team. I'd rehearsed it to the letter, anticipating every question they might ask me. And yet, when I stepped into that room, I felt every eye on me, analyzing my proposal and presence. I delivered and hit every key point, but the response was muted, the same "thank you" that felt perfunctory. Later, a peer presented a proposal with half the preparation, stumbled on several questions, yet walked away with enthusiastic praise. Rule 3 in action: their good enough was remarkable; my flawless execution was just business as usual.

The Mental Toll of Higher Stakes

Let's not sugarcoat it—playing by Rule 3 is exhausting. When you're putting in the work and outperforming, only to watch others receive more recognition for doing less, it can chip away at your confidence. The constant pressure to overdeliver without acknowledgment can make you question whether it's worth it, whether all the extra hours and relentless perfection-ism are achieving anything beyond basic survival.

This is where self-preservation comes in. If you're playing by Rule 3, you must find ways to protect your mental health. That might mean creating your own bench-marks for success or connecting with mentors and allies who recognize your excellence, even if corporate praise is thin. Building a well you can draw from isn't just a nice-to-have, it's essential for a game that pits you at a disadvantage.

Building Your Own System of Validation

The bottom line is this: you can't rely on others for validation. You can't expect the game to hand out recognition equally or assume that your excellence will be rewarded in real time. Instead, focus on setting your own standards of success. Recognize your growth, acknowledge the impact of your work, and find small ways to celebrate your achievements, even if nobody else is clapping. Over time, your accomplishments will speak for themselves, regardless of the recognition you do or don't receive.

Define Excellence for Yourself

In corporate spaces, the bar for you will be set higher, and that's the reality. But your value isn't diminished by the absence of applause or external validation. Excellence isn't a reaction to how others perceive you, it's a reflection of the standards you set for yourself. Keep moving with purpose, let your work be your legacy, and don't let the rules of the game define your worth. Also, don't be afraid to take your talents to a place where they fully recognize what you bring to the table.

Rule 4: There can only be one.

Growing up, I was glued to the TV whenever *Highlander* came on. For anyone who remembers, the premise was simple: There can only be one. One immortal would survive, absorbing the power of all the others. It was thrilling to watch. Who doesn't love a good battle for the top spot? However, years later, when I found myself in the corporate world, that Highlander mentality came back with a new edge. Here, it wasn't about immortals but the unsettling reality that, for Black women, there's often only room for one. One of us is typically allowed at the table, in the department, or on the project, as if our presence is a novelty rather than an asset.

This scarcity model isn't new, though. It's the same mentality Black comics and actresses have spoken about for years—the idea that only one can be "put on" at a time while the rest wait in the wings. Corporate America has applied that same scarcity model with vigor, offering a single, token seat at the table. This seat doesn't expand or multiply, no matter how many of us are qualified to be there. It's tokenism in its most distilled form: a single, symbolic position that meets the "diversity" requirement but denies any true inclusion or equity. And it doesn't just isolate us; it often breeds an unspoken tension. The problem isn't just that the board limits how many of us are allowed in the room. It's that many of us have come to believe this, too. We've internalized it, finding ourselves competing for that seat instead of lifting each other, worried that if one of us advances, there may be no room left for the other.

I saw this firsthand when I transferred into a department where a Black woman was already known as the go-to person for anything technical. She had carved out a solid reputation as the expert in the room. Now, I've always excelled at technology myself. As a solopreneur for years, I'm self-taught on quite a bit of software. Nothing makes me happier than discovering ways to improve a manual or cumbersome process. So even though I've never officially been "IT," my expertise has opened doors—and, at times, been the bane of many an IT person's existence. I don't accept the usual spiel when something isn't working; I come in knowing how things should work and ready with ideas to improve them.

So, when I saw ways to streamline our processes, I shared my ideas, thinking I was helping. But to my surprise, she disagreed, not because the ideas didn't have merit but because they meant changing systems she had put in place. Instead of working together, we found ourselves at odds. Rather than having an ally, the Highlander Mentality and tokenism turned us into reluctant competitors. She saw me as a challenger to her role, and I saw her as someone resistant to change. It was the classic "one at a time" rule playing out before my eyes, a barrier between us that neither of us had created but both of us felt bound by.

Then, there was the Black woman in IT with whom I had to partner for a project where I was the subject-matter expert. The first time we were introduced, she said with a chuckle, "When I think of you, I don't think IT..." It was her not-so-subtle way to tell me that's where I "belonged," as if my ideas on technology had no place at the table because I didn't hold an official IT title. I remember smiling politely, but inside, I was reeling. Instead of seeing me as a potential collaborator, here was someone who saw me as an outsider with no right to weigh in. Every time we interacted, I had to prove myself and justify each recommendation I made—again, as though my presence threatened her standing. Rather than finding common ground, we stayed distant, caught in the lie that stated, "there can only be one." Tokenism made her believe we needed to compete with each other, making it impossible for her to see me as a teammate rather than a threat.

The Burden of Representation

When you're "the one," you don't just carry the expectations of your role but the weight of representation. You're no longer just Nicole in accounting or April in HR. You're the voice, the image, the stand-in for an entire demographic, whether you want that role or not. If you succeed, it's seen as a rare accomplishment. If you falter, it's taken as confirmation that "they" made a mistake, as though the stakes for everyone who looks like you were riding on your performance alone.

This burden can make it hard to move freely, to feel the same ease others take for granted in sharing ideas, taking risks, or even making the occasional mistake. You're always conscious of that invisible "one-and-only" label hanging over you. And with it comes the unspoken reminder that if you're there, it might mean someone else who looks like you won't be.

Why They Keep the Room Small

This "one-at-a-time" mentality isn't accidental. Corporate spaces thrive on a scarcity mindset. If they allow too many of us in, it changes the dynamic, the assumptions, the control. It disrupts the comfort of familiar power structures. And so, they'll hire you, maybe even promote you, but the invitation often stops with you. They'll keep the doors open just enough to claim diversity but not so vast that true equity takes root.

It's also why we often find ourselves in the catch-22 scenario of being the only and, by default, the token. We will get pulled into any project that requires "diversity. " The sadder fact is that most executives will follow this blueprint proudly, patting themselves on the back on just how diverse they are, unwittingly following the same tired charade across the board that makes diversity, equity, and inclusion mostly performative in corporate spaces.

Transforming Isolation Into Influence

The good news is that there's a way you can turn this rule on its head. If you're the one, use that position. Use it to open doors, set a precedent, and be a force for change, even if you must do it subtly. Being "the one" doesn't mean you're alone; it means you're positioned to create a pathway, however small, for those who may come after you. It may mean advocating for policies that promote equity, mentoring other women who are just breaking into the field, or simply showing up in your fullness, unshaken by the scarcity mindset around you.

Yes, they may see only one, but let your work echo so that the next time a hiring decision comes up, they'll remember you as the reason they need more, not fewer, voices like yours in the room.

Beyond the Limits

Navigating Rule 4 requires redefining what success looks like beyond traditional metrics. Your success isn't limited to your promotion or title; it's also in the quiet influence you wield, the examples you set, and the systems you challenge simply by existing within them. The game may feel isolating when you're the one, but isolation doesn't strip you of influence. Even in a room where you stand alone, your impact ripples farther than you realize.

Use "The Rule of One" to Multiply

Let your presence plant the seeds for others in the spaces that try to contain you. Being the one isn't the endgame—it's a starting point. Leverage it, expand it, and create an opening for others to step through when the opportunity arises. While they may only want one, the goal is to leave the door cracked just enough so that, eventually, the one becomes many.

Rule 5: Goalpost's gonna keep shifting.

If you've ever felt like the rules of the game change just as you start to get the hang of them, you're not imagining things. Goalposts are constantly shifting; nowhere is this truer than when you're a Black woman trying to navigate your way up. When you think you've done exactly what's expected, you'll often find that the expectations have changed, the target has moved, and suddenly, what was good enough last week isn't cutting it anymore.

Take it from Viola Davis. Despite being hailed as the "Black Meryl Streep," she has repeatedly pointed out that, unlike her white counterparts, she isn't paid or treated with the same reverence. She's told she's one of the best, given a title that implies respect and admiration, but she's expected to constantly "prove it" without ever seeing the backing to match those words. Admiration of her impressive portfolio doesn't mean access, and appreciation of her phenomenal acting doesn't mean equity. Every accolade comes with an invisible asterisk that says, "Yes, but... show us one more time." It's a constant cycle of validation without compensation, of praise without parity, and for Black women, this "prove-it-again" cycle is all too familiar. This cycle isn't limited to the world of Hollywood; it's something that Black women in corporate America encounter daily.

More Like Her, Less Like You...

The shifting goalposts showed up in my own experience with startling clarity. I remember a conversation with a higher-up, someone I'd gone to for clarity on my growth path after being told repeatedly that I'd "done everything" to position myself for advancement. Instead of providing the direct guidance I sought, they said, "Now, I'm not saying you should be more like [this person], but you should observe what she does and how she conducts herself." He was referring to a white female executive in another department who held the role I aspired to.

Determined to make sense of their advice, I decided to observe her closely, studying her approach and habits, trying to find the missing piece in my trajectory. It didn't take long to realize that the main difference between us — other than the painfully obvious — was that she was deferent to him in a way that I wasn't. She consistently accommodated his perspective, yielding to his authority with each decision in a reverent and almost fearful way, while I was assertive and self-assured. In his view, my growth potential was tied to how willing I was to defer — to be more like the woman who, frankly, had shown her disdain for assertive Black women more than once. A woman who had pushed out or terminated every Black woman who ever had the misfortune to work in her department. So, the guidance was baffling. I was encouraged to emulate not only someone whose methods didn't align with my own but someone who viewed my strength as a shortcoming. Once again, the goalposts shifted beyond my accomplishments to the intangible space of personality and perception.

The Empty Promise

Then, the dreaded departmental reorganization took place. Leading up to this point, I'd taken on additional responsibilities, worked alongside my immediate manager on a transition, and met every curveball thrown my way. My department head was transferred out, and then my immediate manager retired, leaving me as the natural next in line — or so I thought. There was an unspoken expectation that I'd take the reins, and I knew I was ready. I'd put in countless hours, meeting every requirement and exceeding every metric, and I made it known that I was prepared to lead. It seemed like a seamless fit; I was primed, positioned, and had invested time in strengthening my skills.

Instead, the position was given to someone from a different department. And if that wasn't the icing on the cake, I was tasked with training them — guiding this new manager on responsibilities I'd been handling for months. Shortly after the restructuring was announced, my direct reporting line scheduled one-on-one meetings with me. Everyone I spoke to had the same line: "You have done everything you need to do to move to the next level. The rest is up to us." I believed them. I walked away from those conversations feeling validated, assured that all my efforts had been recognized and that a promotion was around the corner. I could see the role right there within reach — the carrot was practically in my hand. And then, just as quickly, it was gone.

When promotion season arrived, it came and went without a word. At the time, it wasn't entirely clear to me that moves and plays were happening behind the scenes that all but assured that promotion would never materialize. When I asked pointedly about advancement, I was told, "Not at this time." Suddenly, I was back at square one, recalibrating for a new direction I hadn't anticipated, with no clear path forward.

This wasn't just disappointing; it was a classic example of the shifting goalposts so many of us face. I'd been told explicitly that my work was enough, that the promotion was in their hands. I'd placed my growth in their hands and trusted their promises. And in doing so, I had handed over the power to shape my advancement. I learned that leaving your future up to someone else's discretion is rarely a sound strategy in corporate America.

Each time I neared the finish line, they moved it a few feet further, forcing me to run harder to keep up. It's the essence of the "prove-it-again" cycle, where simply out- and overperforming aren't enough. Consistency doesn't guarantee stability. Each success, each high-achieving project, is met with a new level I was expected to reach, a fresh "suggestion" to push me further or "improve." On the board, especially as a Black woman, it's not enough to show up and do the work; it's an endless series of hoops to jump through, of targets to hit, only to be met with yet another, often ambiguous, expectation.

It's like a treadmill: no matter how fast or hard you run, you're only ever moving in place. It's not that your work lacks quality; the standards keep evolving, the metrics continually shift, and every achievement becomes a new baseline rather than a point of arrival.

When Progress Isn't Linear

And here's the kicker: progress in corporate spaces is rarely straightforward. Just when you think you've got a path mapped out, something changes, and you're forced to adapt. I can't count how many times I've been told "there's a great opportunity for you here" only for that opportunity to quietly disappear. Promises are made, feedback is given, and you're led to believe that you're on track. But then a reorganization hits, a new manager comes in, or suddenly, the project you were supposed to lead is no longer a priority. You've done everything right, but you're back at square one, readjusting—or in corporate speak, pivoting—in a new direction you didn't ask for.

It's a uniquely frustrating experience when you realize that your upward trajectory depends on a structure built on sand. Promotions that once seemed within reach can vanish as quickly as they appeared, and the sense of accomplishment that comes from reaching your goals is tempered by the realization that those goals may not matter in the next quarter's playbook.

Resilience vs. Reinvention

Over time, I've learned that navigating shifting goalposts requires a mix of resilience and reinvention. Being resilient alone won't cut it. Reinvention is about adjusting, evolving, and finding ways to thrive despite the changes. When the goalposts move, it's not always a signal that you're failing. Sometimes, it's a reminder to revisit your own goals, to ensure that you're working toward something that matters to you, not just the next arbitrary milestone.

You can't control the corporate playbook but can control your own. You'll wear yourself out if you're constantly working toward someone else's moving target.

But when you set your own standards and create your own measures of success, those shifting goalposts start to matter a little less.

Play By Your Own Scoreboard

Corporate goalposts are always going to keep moving. It's part of the game. But you don't have to spend all your energy chasing a finish line that someone else is constantly shifting. Play by your own scoreboard. Define success for yourself, set goals that align with your vision, and remember that while they may keep changing the game, you get to decide which goals are worth reaching and, more importantly, where you should pursue them.

Rule 6: Shade is inevitable.

Yes, shade is inevitable, but it's also irrelevant in the grand scheme of things. In corporate spaces, shade isn't just a possibility, it's a given. You will encounter it if you're moving up, standing out, or simply existing with a purpose. Sometimes, it's subtle, like a side comment that makes you pause and wonder if you imagined it: a microaggression, or as I like to call it, a little shade. Other times, it's right in plain sight: a macroaggression so bold it feels like it's broadcasted, major shade. Either way, shade is part of the package, and if you're a Black woman navigating the board, expect it in all its forms, from whispers to full-on cold fronts.

The thing about shade, especially as it's directed toward Black women, is that it often has deep roots. Microaggressions are typically born from stereotypes, unwitting biases, and ingrained assumptions about who we are or how we're "supposed" to be. They're subtle, almost like background noise, until they're directed right at you. Someone might "innocently" ask a question that reveals the underlying bias in their assumptions. Then there are macroaggressions, the overt statements and actions from people who may be consciously uncomfortable with your presence or success. Macroaggressions are louder, unmistakable in their intention to question your place, and they remind you that some people are fundamentally threatened by what you represent.

Some of these microaggressions come from people who may genuinely not know better. For example, Black women's hair has always been a subject of fascination and misunderstanding for some. A colleague once approached me and asked, "So, how do you wash your hair… when it's like that?" She was referring to my microlocs as if my hair type required some exotic or unfamiliar method. I looked at her and said, "The same way you wash yours." At that moment, her curiosity was unmasked as a microaggression—an unwitting one, perhaps, but still, one rooted in a lack of exposure to the diversity of Black hair. This was shade disguised as curiosity, a reflection of the stereotypes that often cast Black women's hair as "different," "unusual," or "high maintenance," labels that subtly imply we don't quite fit the mold.

Compliments with a Side of Doubt

One of the most common forms of shade comes in the form of compliments that aren't compliments. You know the type: the backhanded comment disguised as a "compliment," the "praise" that leaves you feeling more uneasy than uplifted. I remember (more than) once being told, "Wow, you're so articulate!" The assumption in that supposed praise is that my eloquence is somehow unexpected, as though my ability to string a sentence together is surprising. Compliments like that aren't admiration; they remind us that some people still see us through a narrow lens, surprised that we don't fit their stereotype.

Then there's the "Did you really do that?" kind of shade, where your achievements are met with a hint of disbelief. I once had a colleague look at me with genuine surprise after I'd led a successful project and say, "That was all you?" I smiled, said yes, and attempted to move on, but they took that as an opportunity to throw me a pop quiz because when it comes to our abilities, more often than not, the mantra is "never trust, always verify."

The Cold Shoulder from Unexpected Places

I learned that shade isn't always reserved for people outside your demographic. Sometimes, it comes from people who look like you, individuals you expect to be allies. In one role, I encountered a Black woman who had been at the company far longer than I had, and I thought we'd connect right away. But instead of camaraderie, I was met with cool indifference and a subtle dismissal of my ideas. I tried reaching out and engaging her in discussions, but it became clear that my presence made her uncomfortable. In retrospect, I understood it was likely her way of holding onto her territory, of navigating her own insecurities in an environment that didn't encourage multiple voices from Black women. Still, her cold shoulder stung, reminding me that on the board, sometimes we're even pitted against each other, made to believe that shade is a necessary part of survival.

How to Handle Shade with Grace

If I've learned anything, handling shade isn't about reacting to it every time. Sometimes, the most powerful thing you can do is let it slide. The more energy you spend fighting shade, the more it consumes you, pulling you into a cycle of defending your worth instead of focusing on your goals. I've developed my own strategy for handling shade: I acknowledge it privately, maybe even chuckle about it, and then let it go. Not every battle is worth fighting, and not every comment deserves my response. There's a quiet strength in knowing you're on the right path and shade — whether it's a whisper or a storm — can't derail you unless you let it.

It's also helpful to have a few trusted people you can confide in who understand what you're dealing with. A quick venting session, a knowing laugh with a friend, or even a simple "Can you believe this?" moment can be enough to let the tension dissipate. Surrounding yourself with people who genuinely see and support you is invaluable because they help keep you grounded and remind you of the bigger picture when the shade piles up.

But let me be clear in acknowledging that the ability to be unbothered by shade won't happen overnight, and sometimes, you'll be pulled into the gutter with said "shader." The goal is to let it roll off more often than you allow it to faze you. We are still human, after all.

Keep Shining Anyway

The people throwing shade are often re-acting to their own insecurities and their own discomfort with your growth. Don't let their doubts cloud your confidence. Keep shining anyway. You didn't work this hard to dim your light for someone else's comfort. Hold your head high, let your work speak for itself, and remember that every bit of shade thrown your way proves you're leaving a mark.

Rule 7: Ain't nobody coming to save you.

On the board, especially as a Black woman, one of the most brutal truths to accept is that nobody's coming to save you. And this isn't something I was the first to discover. I've seen many Black women discuss this when they find themselves in the thick of things, on the verge of a PIP (performance improvement plan) or, worse, a breakdown. But I wish we discussed this much earlier, right at the outset. We need to know this going in. No mentor, sponsor, or hidden ally is waiting to swoop in and shield you from the more challenging moments or pull you up when the game gets dirty. Sure, you might have supportive colleagues, maybe even a manager or two, who believe in your potential. But at the end of the day, navigating corporate spaces means realizing that you are your own safety net. You've got to be the one holding the line, showing up, and advocating for yourself because nobody else will do it with the same consistency or commitment.

The Corporate Savior Myth

Corporate America loves to talk about mentorship and sponsorship, building a culture of support, and creating paths to success. And while there are real mentors and champions out there, you often have to prove yourself to a degree that others don't. The idea of a corporate savior swooping in to see your potential and help you rise is often an illusion, a fantasy that doesn't align with reality. If you find someone who wants to invest in your growth, chances are they'll expect you to have already done the groundwork, to have shown that you're twice as good, twice as resilient, and twice as prepared as the person next to you. You're always expected to be self-sufficient, even when you're just starting out.

It's like an unspoken understanding that you've got to earn even the most basic level of support. I've seen people promoted because "they showed promise," a vague statement that's rarely applied to us. For Black women, "showing promise" is often replaced with "proving beyond doubt." And by the time we've reached a point where others are willing to back us, we've usually done so much groundwork that the support feels like an afterthought rather than a leg up.

Learning to Advocate for Yourself

Once I realized that no one was coming to save me, I shifted my approach. Instead of waiting for someone to notice my potential, I started making my accomplishments known. I documented my achievements, advocated for the projects I wanted, and ensured my contributions weren't slipping under the radar. It wasn't about arrogance; it was about visibility. I wouldn't let my work quietly disappear into the background while others advanced.

Self-advocacy isn't always easy and may not seem natural at first. You have to learn to ask for what you need and make your expectations apparent. One valuable tip I got from a higher-up was that the first step to getting a promotion is to state that you want a promotion. Waiting around, hoping someone will notice you and hand it to you, will never happen. Stop assuming that good work will speak for itself and start speaking up. That shift will be a game-changer. You don't have to wait for someone else's approval or hope they'll notice your capabilities. Put your own growth in your hands, and make sure your ambitions are front and center, not an afterthought to someone else's agenda.

Setting Boundaries and Standards

Part of saving yourself in corporate spaces means setting boundaries and establishing standards for your treatment. It's learning to say no when projects are dropped on your plate without regard for your capacity and to push back when you're asked to stretch yourself beyond your capacity. Setting boundaries was a way of respecting my own work and ensuring that others respected it, too. There's power in defining what's acceptable and what isn't, in making it clear that you're not here to be taken for granted.

Corporate environments will often take as much as you're willing to give. It's easy to fall into the trap of overextending yourself, thinking that if you go the extra mile, someone will finally acknowledge your effort. But here's the reality: boundaries don't just protect your energy — they establish your value. When you respect your limits, others start to respect them, too.

Building Your Own Network

Another part of self-sufficiency is finding your own network—people who see you, value you, and want to see you succeed. Corporate America might not hand you a mentor, but that doesn't mean you can't find allies. Sometimes, they're in unexpected places: people who share insights, pass along opportunities, or give you an honest heads-up about what's happening behind the scenes. These aren't always people in high positions; sometimes, they're peers who understand the struggle and know what it's like to feel alone in the game.

I learned to build my network and connect with people who could give me honest feedback and weren't afraid to tell me the truth about where I stood and what I needed to work on. They became my sounding board, reality check, and those who helped me stay grounded and focused. And while they might not have been the "saviors" corporate America promotes, they were precisely the allies I needed to keep moving forward.

Champion Yourself

Your power lies in knowing that your growth, goals, and success are in your hands. When you learn to advocate for yourself, set boundaries, and build your network, you no longer need to wait for someone else's validation. You get to create your own path on your terms. It's a freedom that can't be taken away, a power that stays with you no matter where you go.

Mastering the Rules with Purpose

Think of this chapter as your briefing before stepping into the heart of the game. We haven't fully delved into chess analogies just yet, and that's intentional. Before we dive into strategies and tactics, it's crucial to be grounded in the reality of these rules. We must understand the landscape, recognize the patterns, and know the stakes. These rules are the foundational truths of the board, especially for those who navigate it with a unique set of challenges and strengths, or as is the case for Black women, a sharp disadvantage.

As you read through each rule, I hope you recognize familiar moments that reminded you of your journey or helped clarify the complexities you've encountered. These rules are here to steady you and remind you that your moves aren't random. They're part of a broader game where the goalposts may shift, shade may be inevitable, and allies may be few.

In the chapters that follow, we'll get into the thick of it — the actual plays, the strategies, and the calculated moves that will help you navigate this space on your terms. But for now, let these rules anchor you. Because once you know the game's reality, you can start playing with intention, foresight, and power.

Each rule you uncover is a tool for navigating the board with confidence and clarity. Knowing the rules is about understanding the game well enough to play it your way.

Key Takeaways

- ❖ Know the Rules, Choose Your Moves: Every rule you recognize is a tool that empowers you to respond, adapt, or challenge dynamics that would otherwise limit your potential.
- ❖ Observe Patterns and Build Insight: Consider how these rules play out in your environment. Documenting patterns helps you anticipate challenges and opportunities.
- ❖ Stay Rooted in Your Value: These rules aren't a commentary on your worth; they remind you to remain aware, adapt strategically, and never let the game define your confidence.

Food for Thought

- ➢ **Reflect:** Which of the seven rules resonates most with you? Why do you think that is?
- ➢ **Challenge:** This week, pick one of the rules to observe in your workplace actively. How does it play out? Notice any patterns, key

players, or dynamics that reinforce this rule

Nicole S. Palmer

Chapter 2: Learn the Participants

In any game, knowing the players is as important as knowing the rules. This chapter is about understanding the cast of characters you'll encounter on the board: the allies, the adversaries, and the unpredictable wild cards. Here, we'll take a closer look at each type of participant, exploring who they are, why they act the way they do, and what that means for you.

Each section in this chapter breaks down a specific type of participant you're likely to encounter on the corporate chessboard. Every participant has a part to play, from colleagues who seem eager to support you to those who may see your progress as a threat to the managers and executives who hold power over your advancement. As a Black woman navigating this space, recognizing each player's roles, motivations, and behaviors is essential for strategically positioning yourself.

This chapter is your guide to understanding the entire cast of characters. By the end, you'll have a clearer sense of who each player is and how to anticipate their moves, leverage allies, and protect yourself against adversaries. This allows you to play the game with clarity and confidence, equipped with the insights you need to excel.

Understand Participants Beyond Identity

It's essential to recognize that the participants you encounter on the board may come from varied backgrounds, experiences, and perspectives. While Black men and women often share a unique awareness of the biases, challenges, and unspoken rules Black women face, the dynamics we discuss here aren't exclusive to them. Sometimes, allies or adversaries who don't share your identity can still see these obstacles, even if they experience or interpret them differently.

This context is why understanding motivations, rather than just appearances, becomes vital. You may find genuine support from an unexpected ally outside your demographic, someone who recognizes the realities you face and wants to help you navigate them. Conversely, there may be Black men and women who, for their own reasons, maintain the status quo rather than challenge it. By focusing on each participant's role and motivations rather than assuming alignment based on shared identity, you'll be better equipped to navigate the board strategically, making the most of every alliance and maneuvering through every challenge with clarity.

A Hierarchy of Power and Influence

In chess, every piece has its own movement, purpose, and rank. The corporate board is no different, where each role has its unique level of influence and visibility, forming a hierarchy that determines how power flows. At the top of this hierarchy stands the queen, the most versatile and powerful piece, while the pawn — though often underestimated — represents the potential for growth through strategic positioning. Each piece's role on the board reflects distinct challenges and opportunities, especially for Black women navigating corporate spaces.

The pieces in this book are ordered not by personality or individual value but by their level of influence within this structured hierarchy, much like in chess. We begin with the pawn, a piece that symbolizes early career roles with limited influence, yet boundless potential for growth. At the other end lies the queen, a figure of ultimate authority and adaptability. Between these two extremes are other roles, each with their own strengths, limitations, and survival strategies.

The order of the pieces serves as a framework to understand the journey many Black women experience within corporate spaces. While each role has its own set of dynamics, this progression sheds light on the barriers encountered at every stage — from the invisibility often faced at entry-level to the precariousness that can come even as you approach the highest levels of influence. Though these roles reflect a hierarchy of power, they also speak to the resilience and adaptability required to advance through it.

As you read through each role in this chapter, consider how it applies to your experience. The insights here will help you recognize the barriers that may arise at each level, along with strategies to overcome them. By examining each role's unique challenges, this chapter highlights the adaptability and strategic thinking required to move forward confidently and purposefully.

With this foundation, we start with the pawn, examining what it means to hold potential and ambition while navigating the realities of limited visibility and power.

The Pawn: Foot Soldier

In chess, the pawn is often overlooked. It's the least powerful piece in the game, with limited movement and little flexibility. But despite its modest role, pawns are critical in setting the stage for more significant plays. On the board, the pawn or foot soldier holds a similar position, seemingly minor but integral to the organization's daily operations. These are the people who keep the gears of the company turning. Foot soldiers may not have the most eye-catching roles, but they're essential to the company's operations, and if you pay close attention, you'll find they have the power to shape perceptions and even subtly influence your path. Black women in this role face distinct challenges: they may be seen as replaceable, overlooked for promotions, and subject to biases that others may not face. For these women, the path from foot soldier to a position of influence requires navigating additional barriers that often remain invisible to others.

Who They Are

Foot soldiers aren't always support staff. They exist across various roles, from analysts to specialists to junior managers. They execute the day-to-day work, implement policies, and keep projects on track. While they may not sit in the C-suite, foot soldiers are often the first to see shifts in the company culture or notice changes in priorities long before they're formally announced. And if you're a Black woman navigating corporate spaces, recognizing the importance of these individuals is crucial. These people may not hold titles of power, but they have knowledge, influence, and an ear to the ground — often noticing the dynamics and details unseen by others.

Overlooking their impact would be a mistake. These foot soldiers can quietly set the tone, influence team morale, and shape perceptions, often without realizing the weight of their influence. Think of them as the company's network of ground-level operatives — connected to the daily flow of information. They may not have formal decision-making authority, but they can quietly influence the larger currents of the organization.

The foot soldier role can be fraught with complexity for Black women who are navigating an unspoken hierarchy that can limit their influence. These women may encounter colleagues who expect compliance rather than innovation from them, subtly sidelining their contributions. To be effective as a foot soldier, Black women must excel at their tasks and build strategic relationships that can help them break out of the limitations typically assigned to this role.

How They Operate

In chess, pawns move slowly, one square at a time, and can't go backward. Similarly, foot soldiers tend to operate within defined boundaries and may have limited upward mobility, advancing only when they've put in significant time and effort. However, as in chess, foot soldiers have a potential that is easy to overlook in the corporate realm. When a pawn reaches the far end of the board, it can transform into any piece — often becoming a queen. This journey across the board mirrors the potential for foot soldiers to rise through the ranks and grow from humble beginnings into influential roles. For Black women especially, this serves as a reminder that the journey to power and impact can start from any position, no matter how modest it might seem, given the right circumstances.

That said, foot soldiers can also become literal pawns — manipulated by those with greater power. Some may be tools to advance agendas, control narratives, or influence perceptions. This manipulation isn't always blatant; it can be as innocuous as positioning a foot soldier to steer team dynamics or using their access to control the flow of information. For Black women, understanding this dynamic is key. Sometimes, someone else's motives may shape your interactions with a foot soldier. Learning to read these nuances helps you recognize when a foot soldier's behavior is authentic or when a third party may influence it.

In this role, Black women are vulnerable to manipulation to achieve specific outcomes, to serve a purpose they aren't always fully aware of. This might manifest in being positioned as the "face" of diversity while lacking real influence or being asked to take on additional tasks with promises of advancement that never materialize. Recognizing when someone else's agenda is at play helps foot soldiers maintain autonomy and avoid becoming unwitting participants in dynamics that don't serve their growth.

The Unseen Challenges of the Pawn Role

For Black women, the foot soldier role often entails managing not only the workload but also the microaggressions, biases, and undermining behaviors that come with being in an entry-level- or mid-level position. These women might face assumptions about their capabilities, have their contributions minimized, or even see others take credit for their work. This reality creates a precarious environment where they must constantly prove their worth while battling against stereotypes that others might not even notice. The burden of excellence and the pressure to perform without missteps can make the journey from pawn to a higher role feel exhausting and, at times, isolating.

Role on the Board

Though they may seem passive or peripheral, foot soldiers play a role in the organization's ecosystem and influence others' perceptions and attitudes. Treating them as allies rather than bystanders can make a difference in how smoothly you navigate your workplace interactions. Respecting their place on the board reinforces that every piece, no matter how minor it may seem, has a role and a power that shouldn't be underestimated.

Black women in the foot soldier role have an opportunity to create allies and build a support system that values their contributions, while also safeguarding themselves from exploitation. Recognizing the potential influence of these roles can help Black women leverage their positions to gain the insights and alliances that will aid their long-term journey.

Rule Insights

Rule 3: Their best is your mediocre. Foot soldiers often feel this acutely, particularly Black women who find that their hard work is expected rather than celebrated. In environments where their contributions are taken for granted, Black women may feel the weight of this rule more than others. Understanding the dynamics of the foot soldier role helps them navigate expectations and find ways to make their contributions visible, even if the spotlight isn't always on them.

Rule 5: Goalpost's gonna keep shifting. Foot soldiers frequently see shifting priorities and expectations, often being the first to feel the impact of new directives or policy changes. For Black women, these shifting goalposts can amplify the feeling of instability, requiring constant adaptability while others are afforded more grace. Observing how the foot soldier role adapts to these shifting goalposts can offer insight into the larger corporate landscape, providing valuable lessons on resilience and adaptability in navigating constantly evolving expectations.

Strategy for Success

Engaging effectively with foot soldiers requires respect, authenticity, and strategic foresight. Fostering trust and collaboration can unlock their potential as allies and give them valuable insights into the workplace.

- ✓ Respect their role: Acknowledge the contributions of foot soldiers, even if their titles don't seem to command any obvious authority. Their insights and influence can shape the tone of a department or team.

✓ Show genuine appreciation: Recognize their hard work with small gestures, such as verbal acknowledgments or sincere conversations, to build goodwill and rapport.

✓ Engage sincerely: Take the time to listen to foot soldiers and show interest in their perspectives, fostering trust and collaboration.

✓ Build strategic alliances: Develop relationships with foot soldiers who can serve as allies, providing support and valuable insights into organizational dynamics.

✓ Leverage their observations: Recognize that foot soldiers are often the first to notice changes in company culture or priorities. Pay attention to their observations to stay ahead of potential shifts.

✓ Foster mutual respect: Treat them with dignity and fairness, creating a foundation of trust that encourages them to share tips or heads-ups when challenges arise.

Nicole S. Palmer

✓ Recognize their potential: If treated well, foot soldiers can become critical partners, offering early warning signals and support during challenging times.

For Black women, it's also critical to remain aware of the potential for foot soldiers to act under others' influence. Be discerning in these relationships, recognizing that while foot soldiers can be valuable allies, they may also carry the motivations of those who wield power over them. Building a network of genuine supporters within this group provides useful insights and a foundation of allies who may help you navigate the game with subtle strength and resilience.

The King: Gatekeeper

In chess, the King is the piece around which the entire game revolves. It isn't the most powerful on the board, but its capture dictates the game's outcome. In corporate America, the gatekeeper plays a similar role, controlling access to critical opportunities, resources, and networks. This person may not hold the highest-ranking title, but their influence is profound. The gatekeeper's choices can open doors — or close them just as quickly.

Who They Are

Gatekeepers can be found across various roles and ranks, often in places where their titles don't immediately suggest their influence. A classic example is the administrative or executive assistant to a high-ranking executive. Although their role might seem unassuming, these individuals frequently wield significant influence over who gains favor with those they support.

Underestimating a gatekeeper's power can be a costly mistake.

For Black women, the challenge with gatekeepers can go beyond proving competence; it can involve overcoming unconscious biases or stereotypes that may affect the gatekeeper's perception of who is "worthy" of their support. While some gatekeepers may be open-minded and willing to offer assistance, others might consciously or unconsciously subscribe to a "one-at-a-time" mentality, seeing only limited room for Black women in influential positions. This can create a situation where the gatekeeper subtly withholds opportunities, believing they're already supporting one Black woman or feel unsure about challenging the status quo by sponsoring another. This makes understanding the gatekeeper's values and navigating these nuances critical for Black women.

I first encountered a gatekeeper early in my career, and it quickly became apparent that her influence extended far beyond her title. She wasn't a department head or a senior manager, but she controlled decisions that could propel or hinder a career — often without ever stepping into the spotlight. I learned to observe how they moved within their role and how they valued loyalty, directness, and respect. By showing them how our values aligned, I earned their trust — not by demanding it or being disingenuous, but by recognizing the weight of their position and treating it accordingly.

Whether it's securing project approval, connecting you to influential networks, or recommending your name to key executives, gatekeepers are the unassuming forces shaping careers behind the scenes. Recognizing their power and knowing how to approach them is essential for navigating your path.

How They Operate

In chess, the King moves slowly — one square at a time, with deliberate caution. Similarly, the gatekeeper's moves in the corporate world are subtle and intentional. They don't make swift or bold decisions and rarely openly reveal their full influence. Instead, their actions are measured, quietly determining who gains access to critical spaces and who remains on the periphery.

Gatekeepers are often guarded, extending trust only after observing someone's character over time. They're also acutely aware of their power, usually reacting strongly to any slight or disrespect. One colleague learned this lesson the hard way when he dismissed an executive assistant as "lowly," assuming her rank reflected her power. Little did he know, she was deeply trusted by her executive and heavily influenced everything from opportunities to terminations. After crossing her, he found himself without a role, blindsided by the quiet yet decisive leverage she wielded. That experience reinforced the importance of treating everyone with respect, especially those whose power isn't obvious.

For Black women, interactions with gatekeepers are often a balancing act between asserting oneself and managing perceptions. A single misstep — whether real or perceived — can be enough for a gatekeeper to shift from ally to adversary. Many gatekeepers are accustomed to being subtly "courted" for their influence and may view assertiveness from a Black woman as overstepping. As a result, Black women, in particular, may need to approach gatekeepers with both confidence and deference, showing respect for their position without seeming overly eager or insincere. Building this relationship requires patience, subtlety, and a strong sense of timing, as gatekeepers often expect those seeking their support to understand and respect the unspoken dynamics at play.

Role on the Board

In the organization's ecosystem, the gate-keeper is a pivotal figure. They hold the keys to the people, projects, and places that can make or break careers. Building a relationship with the gatekeeper isn't about superficial networking. It's about showing respect for their influence in the organization's structure. Their endorsement can open doors to significant opportunities, while their quiet disapproval can leave you on the outside looking in.

For Black women, gatekeepers can also represent a particular kind of gatekeeping—a blend of support and surveillance. Some gatekeepers might position themselves as allies but hold unspoken expectations for how Black women should "act" to receive their favor, especially if they are fellow Black women. This can create an environment where, even with their support, you may feel pressured to conform to specific standards of behavior or limit how much of yourself you bring into the workplace. Understanding this can help you navigate the line between leveraging their influence and retaining your authenticity, ensuring that any support received doesn't come at the cost of compromising your identity.

Rule Insights

Rule 1: Nobody talks about playing the game. The gatekeeper understands this rule intuitively. They operate silently, holding knowledge and influence over access without openly acknowledging their power. Recognizing how gatekeepers quietly uphold this rule helps us approach them with the same level of subtlety, learning to work within the "unspoken" guidelines that gatekeepers observe.

Rule 4: There can only be one. Gatekeepers sometimes reinforce the scarcity model, choosing who gains access based on their perceptions and biases. Understanding the impact of this rule when dealing with gatekeepers will help you strategically build alliances. Gatekeepers may only open doors for those they view as aligning with the "one-at-a-time" mentality.

Strategy for Success

Navigating a relationship with a gate-keeper requires respect, patience, and strategic alignment. Follow these steps to gain their trust and unlock their support:

- ✓ Respect their role: recognize the gatekeeper's influence and avoid overstepping boundaries. Approach them with patience and humility, understanding the value they bring to the organization.
- ✓ Build trust gradually: demonstrate integrity, reliability, and consistency in your work to establish a foundation of trust over time.
- ✓ Align with their priorities: keep your contributions visible in ways that align with the gatekeeper's goals and values, showing that your success supports their broader influence.
- ✓ Communicate subtly: share your long-term goals in a way that allows the gatekeeper to see your potential without appearing pushy or self-serving.

- ✓ Demonstrate excellence: consistently deliver high-quality work, ensuring your actions reinforce your credibility and value.
- ✓ Understand unspoken rules: pay attention to the gatekeeper's cues and behaviors, recognizing that they may operate based on unwritten expectations.
- ✓ Earn their advocacy: allow the gatekeeper to observe your value before seeking support. Once they trust you, they can become a powerful ally in advancing your career.
- ✓ Don't wait for validation: while earning their trust, continue to advocate for yourself and build relationships with others in the organization to avoid over-reliance on the gatekeeper.

And remember: gatekeepers can be as much a barrier as a bridge. If you encounter one who seems unwilling to open doors, look for other paths. While they're powerful, they're not the only player on the board, and there are ways to maneuver around them if necessary.

By balancing respect for their role with a readiness to seek alternative routes, you maintain agency and ensure that your progress isn't solely dependent on one individual's approval.

The Knight: Accomplice

In chess, the knight moves unlike any other piece on the board. Its L-shaped jump allows it to leap over obstacles, reaching places other pieces can't. On the board, the accomplice is the person who operates similarly — indirectly, often outside traditional channels of influence. They aren't always the most visible or influential person in the room, but their unconventional approach can make them valuable allies. The accomplice is often that colleague or supporter who can access people, conversations, and opportunities you may not reach directly, helping you in quietly strategic ways. Having an accomplice on the board can be particularly vital. They can help circumvent barriers that may otherwise be difficult to overcome due to systemic biases and willful exclusion from influential circles.

Who They Are

Accomplices can be found in various roles and departments. They might be someone from a different team who occasionally pulls you aside to share insights or offer advice. They may be the person who speaks up on your behalf in meetings, puts in a good word behind closed doors, or connects you with contacts you wouldn't otherwise have access to. Accomplices aren't always the loudest voices, but they're profoundly networked and tend to have quiet sway across different areas of the company.

For Black women, accomplices often bridge hidden opportunities and crucial networks that may otherwise feel closed off. These individuals see beyond stereotypes and recognize your value, often in ways others overlook. Their support isn't about public accolades; it's about ensuring you're considered when it counts. Accomplices can be a lifeline in environments where visibility isn't evenly distributed, subtly advocating for you when you're not in the room. This support can make the difference between being sidelined and having a real chance to advance, particularly in spaces where Black women may have to work twice as hard to achieve the same recognition.

Having a fellow Black woman as an accomplice can be incredibly encouraging and affirming. These alliances are often built on a shared understanding of the unique challenges, biases, and microaggressions that Black women face in corporate spaces. When your accomplice shares your lived experience, there's often an unspoken trust and solidarity that can make their support feel even more significant. These relationships can provide a sense of camaraderie, allowing you to exchange not only strategies but also emotional support in spaces where you may feel isolated.

However, alliances with fellow Black women can also bring complexities. Both of you may feel the pressure of Rule 4, "There can only be one," an unspoken scarcity mindset that corporate culture often imposes on Black women, suggesting that there's limited room for more than one at the top. This dynamic can create tension, as your accomplishments might inadvertently be perceived as competition or a threat to each other's progress. To navigate this, it's essential to approach the relationship transparently and reaffirm your mutual goals. When handled with care, these relationships can become powerful partnerships as you work to elevate the other and challenge the scarcity narrative imposed upon you.

When an accomplice is a fellow Black woman, the alliance often involves additional layers of loyalty and mutual protection. She will be more attuned to the subtle forms of bias or exclusion you encounter, allowing her to advocate for you with a level of empathy and insight that others might not have. This support is invaluable but requires a balance of vulnerability and discernment, knowing that you are navigating similar constraints within the organization. A shared understanding of these realities can transform the relationship into quiet resistance, a way to counteract the barriers that often limit Black women's upward mobility.

How They Operate

Knights in chess move in an L-shape, bypassing other pieces to reach otherwise inaccessible squares. Similarly, accomplices operate indirectly. They don't always announce their support publicly or make grand gestures. Instead, they move with stealth and precision, slipping behind the scenes to advocate for you in ways you may not immediately notice. They may mention your name in conversations with senior leaders, share helpful resources, or provide tips about the unspoken dynamics at play in your workplace.

The indirect approach of an accomplice is especially beneficial for Black women, who may face increased scrutiny and skepticism in corporate settings. Rather than drawing overt attention, accomplices can champion your work in ways that elevate your presence without exposing you to potential backlash. This covert advocacy can help counteract the effects of bias, ensuring that your contributions are recognized in rooms where you may not have direct access. For instance, they might position your work strategically in conversations, framing it to resonate with decision-makers while protecting you from potential pushback.

One former colleague became my accomplice in unexpected ways. Although we weren't in the same department, he'd pull me aside after meetings to share context about certain decisions or offer tips on approaching specific leaders. I soon realized he'd been subtly amplifying my presence in rooms where I wasn't always welcome. He'd mention my work in conversations with senior leaders, creating a ripple effect that brought my contributions into focus without my ever having to push for it myself.

Accomplices have a knack for seeing around corners; they know the culture, the people, and the unspoken rules. Their ability to maneuver within the system gives them a unique influence. They don't walk the straight path; they jump, pivot, and sidestep obstacles, often finding ways to help you avoid pitfalls without drawing attention. In environments where traditional pathways to advancement may be closed off, their agility can be a powerful asset.

Role on the Board

Accomplices often help you navigate the unseen barriers, the unspoken rules, and the unwritten expectations. They recognize that the journey for Black women is different, and they're often keenly aware of the additional hurdles you may face. They understand the stakes and operate as an ally without needing to center themselves. They're also the ones who are unafraid to call out discrepancies, offering a level of candidness that can be refreshing and essential in corporate spaces where equity and transparency are rare.

For Black women, accomplices provide access to spaces and knowledge that might otherwise be difficult to reach. They understand that information is power and are willing to share that power with you, whether by revealing the nuances of workplace politics or giving you insights on how to navigate specific personalities. They know when to offer advice, amplify your voice, and quietly steer opportunities in your direction. Their support is unassuming but strategic, giving you a foothold in places where you may still need support.

Rule Insights

Rule 1: Nobody talks about playing the game. The Accomplice understands the unwritten rules and is adept at moving within them. For Black women, who are often kept outside these dynamics, having an accomplice means access to the unspoken norms and backchannels that others take for granted. Their guidance can give you the insight needed to position yourself effectively, helping you see the patterns others may be navigating invisibly.

Rule 3: Their best is your mediocre. The accomplice understands the double standards at play, where the same level of effort and excellence can be praised for some while seen as the baseline for you. They recognize the gaps between the contributions you make and the recognition you receive and work subtly to help bridge that divide. The accomplice acknowledges the extra miles you're putting in by championing your work in private conversations or amplifying your achievements to others. They ensure your dedication doesn't go unnoticed, even if they have to do so indirectly.

Rule 6: Shade is inevitable. The accomplice knows the shade and microaggressions that can arise in the workplace, particularly when you stand out or excel. Often, they have a unique vantage point to witness how others may undercut your efforts or question your place. Rather than stepping into the spotlight, the accomplice operates covertly, offering you insights and strategies to navigate these situations. They understand that sometimes it's about having someone who knows your challenges and can help you counter them with fortitude. The accomplice is a quiet yet strategic supporter, ensuring the shade you encounter doesn't diminish your impact.

Strategy for Success

Working with an accomplice requires a balance of discretion, gratitude, and strategic collaboration. Follow these steps to build trust and maximize their support:

- ✓ Acknowledge their contributions privately: Show gratitude for their efforts, even if their support isn't visible to others. Avoid public recognition that could compromise their discreet approach.
- ✓ Respect their preference for subtlety: Understand that accomplices prefer to work in the background. Avoid putting them in situations where their advocacy could appear self-serving or backfire.
- ✓ Reciprocate strategically: Offer support and share helpful information to establish a mutually beneficial connection, reinforcing the partnership without overstepping.
- ✓ Build trust through discretion: Maintain confidentiality and carefully handle sensitive information, showing respect to their boundaries and approach.

✓ Seek their insights: Accomplices often have valuable knowledge about people and processes. Listen to their perspective and use their insights to navigate challenges and avoid pitfalls.

✓ Be adaptable: While accomplices can be strong allies, stay vigilant if their support shifts. Keep your strategy flexible to address any potential changes in their alignment.

✓ Avoid over-reliance: Strengthen your network beyond the accomplice to ensure your success doesn't depend solely on their advocacy.

✓ Leverage their reach: Use their connections to access opportunities or information that might otherwise be out of reach, but always with respect for their boundaries.

The Bishop: Operator

In chess, the bishop moves diagonally, crossing long stretches of the board in a single move. While it can't cover the entire board like the queen, its reach across one color—light or dark—makes it uniquely strategic. On the corporate chessboard, the operator plays a similar role: they work behind the scenes, wielding influence from the periphery and often overseeing specific areas or initiatives with a high degree of control. The operator isn't usually the face of the organization, but their impact is felt throughout the company. This role is one of subtlety, expertise, and dedication to the organization's continuity and stability—traits that often make Black operators uniquely valuable in maintaining balance within corporate spaces.

Who They Are

Operators are the experts, the specialists, and the strategic thinkers. They often hold titles like department heads, directors, or project leads. Their authority and influence may not be as visible as that of a senior executive, but it's deeply embedded in the organization's structure. They're the ones who make things happen, and they do so with precision and insight. In many ways, they're the architects of company policy, project success, or departmental growth. Their voices carry weight in decisions that shape the company's future, especially in areas requiring steadiness and dependability.

For Black professionals navigating the board, being an operator often comes with an added layer of responsibility. Stability is both a guiding principle and a survival mechanism, something that becomes a conscious choice, not just a personality trait. Operators understand the challenges and unpredictability that can come from being a visible Black leader in spaces where representation is sparse. To them, corporate stability is about advancing the organization and ensuring its contributions withstand scrutiny. Black operators are often hyper-aware of the unspoken pressures on them to perform consistently, maintain credibility, and prove their value in ways others might not have to.

For Black women navigating corporate spaces, recognizing the operators is critical. These people firmly grasp the unspoken rules, the inner workings, and the "why" behind the company's choices.

They're often the go-to person for understanding the company's history and culture, and they can give you a perspective that few others can. The operator may not be positioned to offer you a promotion or set a company-wide policy. Still, their influence shapes your work environment and the dynamics you'll need to navigate to succeed.

Additional challenges for Black women in operator roles. For Black women specifically, operating from the periphery while striving for influence can be fraught with unique challenges. Often, they must tread carefully to avoid being labeled as "too ambitious" or "disruptive" — terms that are seldom applied to their non-Black peers. Their strategic decisions are scrutinized more intensely, with higher standards for proving their expertise and loyalty. In many cases, Black women in operator roles may feel they must continually demonstrate that they are approachable and knowledgeable to be trusted and respected, a dual expectation that demands significant emotional labor.

Black women in these roles often encounter barriers, where their potential to advance to more visible leadership roles is subtly hindered by biases that gatekeepers and other operators may hold. They're entrusted with responsibilities that make them indispensable, yet they may find themselves overlooked when it comes to public acknowledgment or promotion. Navigating these dynamics means constantly proving their value while managing expectations and sometimes building influence in ways that don't threaten others' perceptions of stability.

How They Operate

The bishop's power in chess comes from its ability to control the board from a distance, moving diagonally to connect with pieces others can't reach. Similarly, operators work covertly, maneuvering within their own space but influencing beyond it. They tend to have a defined area of expertise or control—managing a team, leading a division, or overseeing a critical project—and their moves are calculated and strategic. They may not speak loudly, but when they do, people listen.

Operators also recognize the importance of continuity. Their influence is often based on their steady presence and commitment to the organization's long-term goals. They're strategic in choosing their battles, knowing when to lean in and when to step back. Black operators, in particular, understand that their path to influence may differ from others. For them, stability becomes a personal strategy, creating a space where they can contribute meaningfully without becoming the center of unnecessary attention. They're strategic in balancing assertiveness and approachability, blending excellence with caution that ensures they are seen as trustworthy and consistent.

Operators have a gift for understanding the company's culture, the strengths and weaknesses of its people, and the unspoken expectations that shape the organization. They see the bigger picture and often know the nuances of each team member's role, strengths, and vulnerabilities. Their influence is profound, and they're adept at pulling the strings, ensuring that initiatives align with the company's larger goals. Operators are typically loyal to the institution, sometimes even more than to individual team members, which makes their support valuable but also conditional.

Because they're strategically aligned with the company, operators reward those who understand the game and respect the established structure. For Black women, this can mean balancing the need to respect their authority and prove their value within their framework. Operators respect consistency, expertise, and dedication; they value individuals who understand the long game and don't just seek quick wins.

In the latter half of my career, I was fortunate to have a senior colleague who embodied everything an operator should be: wise, observant, and direct. They weren't the type to show their support publicly, but they helped me avoid pitfalls that would have been easy to stumble into, especially in an environment that wasn't always welcoming.

I was dealing with a challenging management situation, a toxic supervisor who constantly undermined my work.

My colleague gave me pointers on handling it, helping me approach the problem differently. They didn't dismiss my experiences or sugarcoat things; instead, they provided an objective perspective that helped me see both the pitfalls and the possibilities. They became a sounding board when I needed it most, offering candid advice rooted in their deep understanding of the company's dynamics.

There was one instance where I was interested in transitioning to a new role that seemed promising. My colleague, however, cautioned me that it was more of a transient position, unlikely to provide long-term security. Their insight proved invaluable; the role was eliminated after the project wrapped up. By listening to their advice, I avoided a career setback and learned the importance of reading between the lines.

Their support not only helped me navigate immediate challenges but also shaped how I approached the work itself. I started to read nuance better, to listen more, and to speak with intention. While our rapport wasn't apparent to everyone—just as they preferred — it reinforced my confidence, knowing someone respected my abilities and saw my potential. This operator saw my value and even tapped me for projects others might not have, a quiet endorsement that spoke volumes.

Black women as operators often have to deploy their influence more subtly, ensuring that their guidance or contributions do not overshadow those of others who may hold more visible roles. This usually requires a nuanced understanding of the company's internal politics, and the unspoken expectations placed upon them. By positioning themselves as reliable problem-solvers and experts, Black women in this role can build beneficial alliances and gain the respect of colleagues. Yet, they may still find that their contributions are sidelined regarding visible credit.

Role on the Board

In corporate settings, the operator is the linchpin whose opinion matters in closed-door discussions. Others often turn to them for advice on executing a new policy, resolving team conflicts, or understanding the nuances of a specific project. They don't usually seek the spotlight but are at the table, weighing in on decisions impacting the organization's future.

For Black operators, maintaining this role can mean carefully navigating perceptions and proving that their choices are in the company's and career's best interests. They must earn credibility without appearing too assertive, remain accessible without compromising their boundaries, and adapt to shifting dynamics while staying rooted in their expertise. This balancing act is critical, as Black operators often face unique challenges in being perceived as influential and approachable without overextending themselves. Their support provides strength and stability, especially when the environment becomes uncertain.

Having an operator as an ally can open doors in unexpected ways. A nod of approval from an operator can earn you credibility across the company. However, operators aren't swayed by charm or surface-level rapport. To gain their support, you'll need to show that you're in it for the long haul — that you understand the company's needs, bring expertise to the table, and are committed to contributing to the organization's success.

But there's a caution here: operators can also become obstacles if they view you as a disruptor or feel that you don't respect the existing order. They have a strong sense of what works and what doesn't and are not shy about reinforcing boundaries to maintain stability. Their loyalty is typically to the system itself, and they may see anyone who challenges it as a risk rather than an asset.

Rule Insights

Rule 1: Nobody talks about playing the game. Operators are masters of the unspoken rules, often working quietly behind the scenes to maintain the corporate balance. For Black operators, this involves a unique level of awareness and adaptability, understanding that their moves are constantly being observed. By aligning their strategies with the organization's unspoken expectations, they ensure their influence remains steady and respected across the board.

Rule 3: Their best is your mediocre. Operators see how double standards affect you and may either reinforce or challenge this disparity depending on their values and biases. They know that competence doesn't guarantee recognition, especially for Black women. Your ability to meet elevated standards can resonate with those who respect quality and consistency, making them more inclined to offer their support or at least respect your dedication. Understanding this rule's impact on your day-to-day can help you tailor your interactions with operators, showing them that you're prepared to deliver, even when the bar is set higher for you.

Rule 5: Goalpost's gonna keep shifting. Operators know the shifting goalposts intimately — they're often involved in setting or adjusting them. They also understand that, particularly for Black professionals, these shifts can sometimes reflect biases or pressures that others don't experience. By remaining steady and focused on long-term objectives, operators ensure they adapt to these shifting standards without compromising their core values.

Rule 6: Shade is inevitable. Operators aren't strangers to the subtle politics and shade that come into play in corporate spaces. They often navigate these dynamics, albeit with a unique blend of discretion and control. When they see you encounter shade, they're likely to recognize it, even if they don't openly acknowledge it. If cultivated wisely, this shared understanding can foster a subtle but powerful respect. Demonstrating awareness of shade while not allowing it to derail you can build credibility with an operator, showing them that you grasp the nuances of corporate survival.

Strategy for Success

Engaging with an operator requires patience, strategic thinking, and respect for their expertise. Follow these steps to build rapport and secure their support:

- ✓ Build rapport gradually: Approach operators thoughtfully and with respect for their insight. Take the time to understand their role and perspective before seeking their guidance or approval.

✓ Recognize their expertise: Acknowledge their contributions and seek their input on issues that matter to your work, showing that you value their knowledge.

✓ Ask intelligent questions: Come prepared and ask well-informed questions demonstrating your understanding of the organization and its long-term goals.

✓ Deliver consistent results: operators respect commitment and performance. Focus on building your reputation by consistently delivering high-quality work.

✓ Align your goals with organizational priorities: Highlight how your objectives align with the company's overarching strategy, proving your value as a team player.

✓ Seek their advice strategically: Involve them in crucial projects or decisions by asking for their perspective, which can help foster mutual respect and build trust.

- ✓ Acknowledge their contributions publicly: Subtly credit their influence or guidance in group settings to reinforce your appreciation without overdoing it.
- ✓ Demonstrate resilience: operators are observing how you handle challenges and setbacks. Show adaptability and a long-term focus, avoiding overt displays of short-term ambition.
- ✓ Be strategic in timing: Don't rush to secure their support; operators often play the long game. Be patient and consistent in your efforts to earn their trust.

And remember: operators are rarely impressed by short-term ambition. They're thinking strategically, watching how well you adapt, how you handle setbacks, and whether you understand the nuances of the game. If you can gain their trust and respect, their support can provide a foundation that helps you weather challenges and secure opportunities.

The Rook: Player

You may have noticed by now that I've intentionally ordered these pieces. The pieces in this book are ordered by rank of power, with the player representing the penultimate role of influence just below the queen. Many ambitious Black women occupy this level, well-positioned within their organizations yet facing systemic barriers that others don't encounter. This section sheds light on what it takes to excel in this role and avoid the traps that can keep you from advancing further...

The rook is a powerful chess piece, moving in straight lines across the board. It's often positioned in the corners, standing as a stronghold that commands control over long stretches of squares. On the board, the player mirrors this role: they're the ones who move decisively, strategically, and often within the confines of clear rules. They are usually well-established, highly visible, and play by straightforward tactics that bring stability and strength. The player can be an ally who supports your moves or, depending on their motivations, a competitor who leverages their power to maintain control.

Players have climbed the ranks through hard work and skill, building a reputation as a reliable, consistent presence. But this stability is deceptive—it's more precarious than it seems, particularly for Black women. For all their accomplishments, many Black women find themselves stalling out at the Player level, blocked by biases, microaggressions, and shifting standards that make it challenging to reach the pinnacle of influence.

Who They Are

Players typically have carved out a solid position within the organization. They may be senior managers, directors, or long-term employees who are trusted and respected. They tend to be direct and predictable and operate within established norms. Their power doesn't come from subtle maneuvers or covert influence—it's clear, visible, and often linked to their years of service, relationships with other key figures, or expertise in a specific area.

Players are reliable. They're the ones who understand the organizational landscape and operate with confidence, often upholding the existing structure. They're not generally interested in challenging the status quo but in maintaining the stability they've worked hard to achieve. This can make them solid allies, as they're usually straightforward and open about their goals and methods. However, if they see you as a threat or someone who disrupts their well-defined space, they can use their influence to push back.

For Black women in corporate spaces, recognizing the Player is essential. These individuals often control specific departments or initiatives and have a significant say in who moves forward and who doesn't. They're well-connected and may not be as subtle as other pieces, but they're respected. Understanding their goals and positioning yourself as an asset to their objectives can help you navigate their influence effectively.

I was in a player role for the better part of my corporate career. Every role, promotion, and lateral move was a deliberate choice to achieve a larger vision. For example, I accepted a position in a new department that didn't seem like a promotion but offered exposure and skills I knew would be critical for a higher-level role. That "sideways" move became a stepping stone for advancement within a year. Players often make such strategic moves, recognizing that power sometimes comes not from immediate gain but from positioning oneself wisely over time.

The Precarious Reality of Being a Player

While the player role can be one of power and influence, it often feels like walking on a tightrope for Black women. Despite their capabilities, they may find themselves sidelined, their accomplishments minimized, or their ideas attributed to others. This phenomenon isn't incidental; it's rooted in deep-seated biases that view Black women's contributions through a harsher, more skeptical lens. As a result, Black women in the player role frequently experience:

❖ Microaggressions: Comments and actions that subtly undermine their authority, expertise, or even their right to be in the room. These can range from colleagues questioning their decisions to supervisors "forgetting" to credit their work.

❖ Sidelining and Underestimation: Players often find that their ideas are only acknowledged when voiced by others or that their career development is slowed despite a consistently strong performance. Unlike their peers, they may be bypassed for high-visibility projects or strategically essential roles, limiting their chances for growth.

❖ Unreasonable Expectations: The standards are often higher, with Black women required to perform at a level of excellence just to be seen as competent. Where others might be given the benefit of the doubt, Black women must constantly prove their worth. This "prove-it-again" bias can lead to burnout and a sense that they're perpetually being evaluated, with little room for error.

This experience of being visible yet undervalued can be exhausting and demoralizing. The Player role becomes a paradox: influential enough to be noticed but not always valued enough to be trusted with actual authority. These barriers make it easy to stall out at this stage, unable to advance to the Queen level despite having the skills and ambition to do so.

How They Operate

Rooks in chess move in straight lines, and the player similarly operates with directness and clarity. They're typically transparent about their intentions, making them predictable allies or competitors. Players like structure and tend to support those who play by the rules. Their influence is powerful yet contained — they don't stray from the familiar paths, preferring strategies with a proven track record.

In corporate settings, players are usually vocal in meetings, assertive about their opinions, and unafraid to advocate for their team or department. Their moves are deliberate and visible, and they tend to command respect in group settings. You can usually tell where you stand with a player because they don't rely on subtlety or hidden agendas. However, if they feel threatened, they'll often act decisively to protect their position and won't shy away from making their boundaries known.

Because players value consistency and predictability, they may not always be the first to support disruptive ideas or untested approaches. For Black women, this can mean needing to "prove" traditional competencies before introducing new perspectives. However, once you've demonstrated your reliability, players can become dependable allies who advocate for you openly, even if they may not initially take risks on your behalf.

Role on the Board

On the board, players are the backbone of many organizations. They may not hold the highest-ranking titles, but they command respect and considerable influence within their departments. These are the people who have often built solid and lasting relationships within the company, and their opinions can carry weight in hiring decisions, promotions, and team dynamics. They're known for their reliability; others often rely on them to uphold the organization's standards.

Players aren't typically interested in taking risks that might destabilize their role or the structure they're part of. However, they're invaluable when you need someone to advocate for the stability of a project, enforce clear standards, or ensure that tasks are completed efficiently. Having a player in your corner means having a steady source of support that can provide credibility and influence in areas where consistency is valued. Conversely, suppose a player sees you as a threat to their position or their cultivated stability. In that case, they may use their influence to stall your progress, especially if they feel you're pushing against the established norms they value.

Rule Insights

Rule 4: There can only be one. The player role is often inhabited by someone who has firmly secured their place within the company. However, they may unconsciously believe there's room for only one "go-to" person within their space. This mindset can create tension if they view you as a rising threat to their established position. Recognizing this dynamic can help you approach the player as a potential ally rather than a competitor. It allows you to sidestep the "one-at-a-time" trap and find ways to complement their influence.

Rule 5: Goalpost's gonna keep shifting. Players are familiar with shifting expectations, as they've likely had to adjust their goals and roles to maintain their status over time. In their commitment to stability and structure, they may unintentionally uphold moving standards, making it challenging for others, especially Black women, to gain consistent recognition. Understanding this tendency allows you to approach the player strategically, showing your adaptability and aligning yourself with their vision without being overtly dependent on their validation.

Rule 7: Ain't nobody coming to save you. As someone who has often navigated corporate landscapes without an apparent safety net, the player knows what it takes to stay relevant. They appreciate others who advocate for themselves and may even respect you more if you show you can hold your own. By demonstrating self-sufficiency, you can build rapport with the player and establish a relationship rooted in mutual respect, positioning yourself as an equal rather than someone looking for protection or shortcuts.

Strategy for Success

Engaging with a player requires transparency, reliability, and respect for the organization's structure. Use these strategies to earn their trust and support:

- ✓ Be transparent and reliable: Demonstrate consistency in your actions and communication. Players respect colleagues who are dependable and straightforward.

- ✓ Show respect for organizational norms: Understand the frameworks and values they prioritize and operate within those boundaries to build alignment.
- ✓ Demonstrate stability: Avoid unnecessary disruption and show that your approach supports, rather than challenges, the existing structure.
- ✓ Align with their goals: Identify their objectives and emphasize how your work complements and advances their priorities.
- ✓ Speak to their values: Highlight your commitment to quality, consistency, and integrity, which players respect and value.
- ✓ Clarify your intentions: Be clear about your role and purpose, ensuring they see you as an ally, not a threat.
- ✓ Position yourself as a collaborator: Reinforce that you're there to enhance collaboration and add value rather than engage in competition.

✓ Set clear boundaries: Maintain professional limits to prevent misinterpretation of your intentions, ensuring mutual respect.
✓ Stay adaptable: Be prepared to navigate subtle shifts in their demeanor if they perceive a threat and recalibrate to reinforce your role as a supporter.

By aligning with their priorities and demonstrating reliability, you can position yourself as a valuable ally to a player, fostering trust and collaboration.

The Queen: Master

In chess, a master is more than just a player who has dedicated countless hours to studying the game, understanding its nuances, and refining their strategy. Chess masters can anticipate moves before they happen, foresee threats, and adapt their play to whatever challenges arise. In corporate America, the queen, or master, plays a similar role: she's the high-ranking Black female leader who has mastered not only the rules but the

unspoken dynamics, the nuanced decisions, and the unseen obstacles of the
corporate game. She's a leader who has
broken through systemic barriers and
carries a unique weight of expectation
and representation. Her role requires
agility, resilience, and the wisdom to
navigate challenges that often come with
being highly visible and intensely scrutinized. Her experience and insight are unmatched, making her a powerful ally and
a formidable presence on the board.

The queen is the most powerful piece on
the chessboard, able to move in any direction with unmatched versatility and
strength. Similarly, the master holds a
strategic and powerful influence, shaping her surroundings while navigating
challenges with a depth of expertise and
resilience. She is the rare leader who has
broken through stereotypes and reached
a level where her influence is undeniable.
Her presence is both inspiring and formidable. She is proof-positive of what it
means to succeed on one's own terms in
spaces that weren't designed for her.

Who They Are

Masters have earned their power through expertise, resilience, and a track record that speaks for itself. They've reached a level where their reputation precedes them, where respect isn't requested but given automatically. However, for Black women in this role, this respect is often hard-won, and they may still need to prove their capabilities in ways others do not. Their successes are scrutinized more intensely, and their mistakes are remembered longer, creating a double standard they must navigate daily. These women command authority not just because of their titles but because of their impact over the years. They are the first and often only Black woman in their position, carrying their own ambitions and the weight of representation for others who look like them.

For Black women striving to climb the corporate ladder, finding a master who understands your unique path is essential. A master is one of the most important figures you can find. When I met a master, it was too little, too late. I was already deep into my career, facing struggles I might have avoided had I known her sooner. That's my one regret—that I didn't find her earlier. Identifying a master who has already reached the mountaintop you're striving for can make all the difference, helping you see that the journey is possible and that there's someone who genuinely understands your challenges and knows how to navigate them.

The master I encountered was already a seasoned leader who had reached the pinnacle of her profession. She came into our organization not because she needed another title but because she wanted a role that allowed for balance and let her influence extend without sacrificing her well-being. Her presence alone was enough to shift the energy in any room. This woman showed me that mastery isn't about your role; it's about the authority you carry, the authority that transcends titles or settings.

A true master is not born from a single role or responsibility; she has walked the path of every piece on the board, from pawn to queen, with her eyes wide open.

For Black women, this journey is often fraught with barriers that others don't encounter, making the transformation from pawn to queen not only a tale of skill and perseverance but also a defiance of systemic limitations. This journey grants her an unmatched understanding of corporate dynamics, allowing her to anticipate moves, recognize risks, and strategize with a depth of insight that comes only from experience. Each stage has required her to be competent and exceptional, and even then, advance-ment has often come only after proving her value in ways her peers did not have to. She knows what it's like to be the pawn, advancing step by step, the knight, maneuvering through obstacles, and the bishop, influencing from the periphery. This versatility is her strength and forms the foundation of her influence.

How They Operate

The Queen moves freely in chess, covering any square on the board with an unmatched range. Similarly, the master has the versatility to step into various roles — mentor, strategist, advocate — without missing a beat. Yet, unlike her peers, her moves are often carefully calculated, and she knows that a single misstep can be magnified. She is both an asset and a visible reminder of diversity; with that comes heightened expectations and greater scrutiny. She moves with intention, using her position not just for herself but to elevate others around her. Masters in this role often carry the unspoken responsibility of breaking down barriers for those who come after them, and they're acutely aware of the need to succeed not just for their own sake but as a beacon for others.

Her influence is rarely loud or forceful, rooted in a calm confidence that speaks louder than words. She knows the power of presence and wields it gracefully. Masters are the leaders who can sit silently through a meeting and still set the tone. They're given a level of autonomy and flexibility that most Black women rarely experience, yet they carry it without losing sight of what it took to reach that position. Unlike others who might distance themselves from their beginnings, masters remain grounded, aware of how far they've come and what it means to hold space for others.

Breaking Free From the Glass Cliff

For a master to excel, her success cannot hinge on a precarious position known as the "glass cliff." Unlike many high-ranking Black women promoted to lead during organizational crises, the master's value lies in her consistent, strategic contributions — not as a last resort in times of trouble. However, even in stable environments, Black women in these roles often encounter a unique set of expectations. They are called upon to lead diversity initiatives, to represent change, and to bring "innovation" in ways that others may not be asked. This expectation to continually "prove" their value can be exhausting and limiting, narrowing the scope of their role even as they rise. Her mastery is most effective when her role reflects the organization's commitment to stability and growth, not crisis management. In this way, her influence becomes a driving force in a thriving environment where her experience is leveraged thoughtfully rather than reactively.

The Power of a Supportive Environment

A master's expertise flourishes in environments where her multidimensional experience is respected and her strategic vision is valued. This supportive environment is rare and precious for Black women, requiring both individual allies and organizational commitment. Genuine support is more than a title or recognition; it's about allowing her to lead without needing to prove her place constantly. To lead effectively, she needs more than just a title — she needs a seat at the table that's not contingent upon saving a sinking ship but is rooted in recognition of her ability. Here, her strength lies not in rescuing the organization but in steering it towards sustainable success. A supportive environment doesn't merely place her in a visible position; it ensures her expertise is acknowledged and her contributions are foundational to the organization's long-term goals.

Role on the Board

In corporate spaces, the master is often a beacon, someone others look up to as proof that it's possible to succeed against the odds. Her visibility and credibility come with a weight that she carries on behalf of all who look like her, consciously or not. She becomes the example, the standard that others are held to, which means that her every move is scrutinized more closely. And yet, she navigates this pressure with ease, using her influence to advocate for change, mentor emerging leaders, and create environments where diverse voices are heard and valued.

The master's presence is often felt before she enters the room. People know her name, her work, her impact. For many, she is a role model not because she's perfect but because she embodies the potential for excellence even when the path is steep. She has proven her value so thoroughly that organizations trust her judgment, even if they don't always understand it. She's achieved respect and freedom that few Black women experience in corporate America, which speaks to her agility, intelligence, and strategic acumen.

Rule Insights

Rule 5: Goalpost's gonna keep shifting. Masters have likely experienced shifting goalposts firsthand, repeatedly required to prove themselves despite their achievements. Their journey to this level of influence is a testament to their resilience and adaptability, even when expectations were unclear or unfairly high. Masters embody the understand-ing that each shifting goalpost is an opportunity to solidify their value, and they do so in a way that creates lasting impact.

Rule 6: Shade is inevitable. Masters didn't reach this level without encountering resistance, and many have spent years working twice as hard to get a place where their worth is no longer questioned. They know the game is rigged, and the rules change constantly, but they've played and adapted long enough to make their own rules. Their presence on the board is a reminder that even when shade is inevitable, success is still possible—and that the ultimate power comes from mastering not just the game but oneself.

Strategy for Success

When engaging with a master or striving to emulate her success, follow these steps:

- ✓ Approach with humility and respect: acknowledge the effort and resilience it took for her to reach this level and show genuine admiration for her journey.
- ✓ Be authentic: avoid trying to impress unnecessarily. Masters value sincerity and authenticity in those they mentor or collaborate with.
- ✓ Seize mentorship opportunities: if offered the chance to learn from a master, embrace it fully, recognizing the rarity and value of her time and guidance.
- ✓ Demonstrate your value: show through your actions that you respect her investment in you by contributing meaningfully and staying committed.
- ✓ Focus on building your reputation: strive to become known for your expertise, integrity, and

ability to influence those around you positively.

✓ Create power, don't chase it: like a master, focus on building lasting impact through skill, integrity, and empowering others.

✓ Show up with intention: approach every interaction and opportunity with purpose, demonstrating your deliberate and thoughtful actions.

✓ Lift others as you climb: emulate the master by supporting others, reinforcing that authentic leadership involves building others up, not just advancing yourself.

✓ Hold your space confidently: exude the quiet self-assurance that comes from knowing your worth and place, regardless of your position on the board.

By respecting a master's journey and embracing her qualities, you gain valuable insights and set yourself on the path to becoming a master in your own right.

The Fluidity of the Roles

All that said, here's the thing about these roles: they're never set in stone. In the game, people shift positions more often than you'd think. Today's foot soldier could become tomorrow's gatekeeper, with access and control you might not have expected. Someone who seems like a pawn in one scenario might hold the keys to critical opportunities in another. Every person on the board can — and often will — move between roles, adapting as situations and strategies evolve. Knowing this allows you to navigate the board with the keen understanding that everyone's role is fluid, including yours.

These roles are dynamic and responsive to the tides of corporate change. What doesn't change, though, is that each piece on the board matters. Whether they're influencing the game with a bold move or making quieter adjustments from the sidelines, everyone you encounter plays a role in how the game unfolds. Success in this environment is about finesse, reading the board, understanding motivations, and aligning yourself in ways as strategic as they are intentional.

Knowing these roles isn't just about labeling the people around you or yourself. It's about equipping yourself with the insight to engage thoughtfully. These archetypes are guideposts, helping you identify who might open doors, who could clear paths, and who might throw up a roadblock. They're the foundation, but remember, the real work is recognizing that each piece can shift and play different parts as the game progresses.

Key Takeaways

- ❖ Recognize Roles, Not Just Titles: Beyond job titles, observe the influence each individual has within the corporate dynamics. Recognizing how people operate within these roles can be more insightful than relying solely on what's printed on a business card.
- ❖ Map Out Alliances and Oppositions: Not everyone in the organization will be an ally, but everyone has a role. Identify who can support, challenge, or block you so you can navigate strategically.

This mapping also helps you anticipate responses to your moves.

❖ Observe and Engage with Purpose: Approach each interaction with curiosity and intention. Take time to understand the motivations and hidden influences that shape your workplace. This purposeful engagement lets you read situations more accurately and respond strategically.

Food for Thought

❖ **Reflect:** Who in your workplace is most influential, and why? Consider whether their influence stems from relationships, expertise, or information access and how they maintain this position over time.

❖ **Challenge:** This week, identify one influential person to observe closely in a team setting. Pay attention to how they communicate, the moments they choose to assert themselves, and the responses they elicit from others. Consider what you can learn from their approach to enhance your influence.

Chapter 3: Study the Board

Imagine stepping onto a chessboard mid-game. You don't know the moves that brought the board to this exact setup, but you know enough to realize one thing: you must study the board before making a move. Understand every square, every piece, and every invisible line of power that runs across it. In the workplace, this same principle applies. The dynamics, hidden alliances, and whispered influence must be studied before you even think about making your next move. Ideally, you're doing this at the outset of your new role rather than midway through, but if you're already in the thick of it, there's no time like the present.

The rules we covered? Those are your foundation. Applying them in real time? That takes knowing the terrain. This isn't passive observation; it's watching with purpose.

The Power of Observation

Just like each square on a chessboard opens up different possibilities, every team, department, and interaction in your workplace has its dynamics and expectations. Observing these dynamics goes beyond knowing titles or job descriptions. It's about paying attention to the nuances. Who truly has influence? Who's quietly making decisions behind the scenes? And who's just a bystander for now, waiting for their moment?

For Black women, studying the board often means looking deeper than the surface-level hierarchy. You're identifying the key players and recognizing the unwritten expectations and biases that influence how each person moves. Who gets to be seen as a leader without question? Who has to prove themselves repeatedly? And where do you fit in the mix?

When I first stepped into a senior role, I quickly learned that titles often didn't align with actual power. I shared the same management position as a colleague who embodied the stereotypical "polished and presentable" ideal that our supervisor and other top executives seemed to favor. While I was responsible for the bulk of the work—shouldering the critical tasks that kept projects moving forward—she was consistently positioned to showcase that work publicly.

Rather than taking on equal responsibility, she benefited from my efforts, presenting my work as her own and gaining visibility I wasn't afforded. Her access to our supervisor's favor allowed her to encroach on areas I managed without having to handle the day-to-day details. Watching this dynamic play out taught me more about the actual power structure than any organizational chart ever could. This observation helps you identify roadblocks and see where your energy is best spent.

Rule Insights

Rule 5: Goalposts Gonna Keep Shifting. In corporate environments, the criteria for recognition can change frequently. Observing which roles retain influence even as goals shift allows you to position yourself effectively, building a steady foundation even when the spotlight moves.

Strategy for Success

To position yourself strategically while navigating the workplace, follow these steps:

- ✓ Observe actively but discreetly: Pay attention in meetings and conversations to identify key influencers and understand the unspoken rules of the organization.
- ✓ Take detailed notes: Document dynamics and interactions to uncover patterns and insights that can help you navigate effectively.
- ✓ Avoid overexposure early on: Like in chess, occupying a central position is valuable, but overextending yourself too quickly can leave you vulnerable.
- ✓ Seek roles that align with your strengths and values: Choose positions that allow you to contribute in ways that resonate with your skills and principles.
- ✓ Look for cross-functional projects: Participate in initiatives that

showcase your impact across departments without placing you directly in the spotlight.

✓ Prioritize strategic positioning over titles: Seek roles that place you where you can have an impact and be noticed by key decision-makers without unnecessary visibility.

✓ Adapt to shifting priorities: Stay flexible and align your efforts with the organization's evolving needs to ensure your position remains relevant.

✓ Leverage subtle visibility: Build relationships and demonstrate value quietly, allowing your work to speak for itself rather than chasing constant recognition.

✓ Balance effectiveness with discretion: Strive to maintain a balance where you contribute meaningfully while protecting your autonomy and reputation.

Strategic positioning is about making intentional choices, contributing in ways that highlight your unique value, and aligning your work with organizational needs—all while maintaining a low-risk but high-impact presence.

Anticipate Moves: Seeing Patterns on the Board

A seasoned chess player doesn't just see the current board, they predict what's coming. In the workplace, this means keeping an ear out for shifts in leadership, industry trends, and evolving company goals. It's about thinking beyond your immediate role and positioning yourself for the change you sense is coming.

In many cases, Black women don't get the luxury of waiting to be invited to the table. We need to recognize trends and plan our strategies accordingly, sometimes even before official plans are made public. By learning to see patterns—whether it's the kinds of projects that earn visibility or the shifts that signal leadership changes, you position yourself as someone ready to pivot. That way, you're not just surviving in an environment that changes on a whim but preparing yourself to thrive in it.

Rule Insights

Rule 7: Ain't nobody coming to save you. In a world where workplace changes are often sudden, relying on your own foresight is essential. Observing patterns and anticipating shifts puts you in a proactive stance, reducing your dependence on others for guidance or rescue.

Strategy for Success

To anticipate moves and recognize patterns in the workplace, follow these actionable steps:

❖ Stay informed on industry trends: Regularly read industry news and reports to understand broader patterns and anticipate potential changes that may impact your role or organization.

❖ Monitor company announcements: Pay attention to internal updates, leadership changes, and organizational shifts to stay ahead of the curve.

❖ Observe critical projects and priorities: Identify the types of initiatives or tasks that gain visibility and align your contributions with those areas.

❖ Build foresight through connections: Engage with colleagues and mentors who have a pulse on company direction or industry trends to gather valuable insights.

❖ Position yourself for upcoming opportunities: Use the knowledge you gain to strategically align your skills, projects, and network to remain adaptable and ready for change.

❖ Proactively prepare for pivots: Create a flexible career plan that allows you to adjust your focus and priorities as new opportunities, or challenges arise.

By cultivating foresight and staying proactive, you'll place yourself in a position of strength, ready to thrive in an ever-changing environment.

Who's Backing Whom?

Alliances are a delicate dance in corporate America, and I learned early on that understanding them is half the battle. For context, I have an obsession with MTV's

The Challenge. If you've watched even a single season, you know alliances are the game's bedrock. The Challenge brings together competitors from various reality shows to battle it out through intense physical and mental challenges, all hoping to win a massive cash prize. But the challenges themselves? That's only half the game. The other half, which makes or breaks players, is the alliance formed behind the scenes.

On *The Challenge*, alliances decide who gets sent into elimination rounds, who stays safe, and who's got a target on their back. And it doesn't stop there. There are alliances within alliances, betrayals, and players shifting loyalties based on what will best serve them. Watching those moves taught me something powerful: alliances aren't static, and not every alliance is as it appears on the surface. Some are strategic partnerships, while others are setups waiting to happen.

Corporate America operates with a similar logic. Alliances here may not be as obvious or cutthroat, but they hold the same weight. Maybe you notice two colleagues who always back each other up in meetings or a manager who quietly champions someone's ideas. Then there are those alliances within alliances, the informal groups that gather after hours or the side conversations happening right before a big decision. Learning to see these alliances, to watch who's aligned with whom, is vital to understanding the dynamics that shape your path forward.

Recognizing alliances keeps you from falling prey to surprises and can show you where to find potential allies — or spot hidden adversaries.

Rule Insights

Rule 4: There can only be one. In environments where opportunities for advancement are limited, alliances can become rivalries. By understanding who backs whom, you can identify authentic relationships and avoid getting drawn into competitions that don't serve your goals.

Strategy for Success

Corporate alliances may not be as overt as those on a reality competition show, but they hold as much weight in determining who rises, falls, and gets left in the background.

- ✓ Identify alliances: Pay attention to colleagues who consistently collaborate or advocate for each other.
- ✓ Evaluate relationships: Observe how alliances affect meeting dynamics, decisions, and promotions.
- ✓ Build your alliances: Align with individuals who share your values and goals to create meaningful partnerships.
- ✓ Avoid unnecessary rivalries: Be selective in choosing which alliances to engage with, focusing on those that advance your long-term objectives.

Understanding alliances is more than just noting who works well together — it's about seeing the undercurrents that influence decisions and outcomes. By building and aligning with strategic allies, you position yourself as someone who understands the game and the players behind it.

Spot the Power Squares

In chess, certain squares hold the most strategic value. The board is no different. These "spaces" aren't always front-and-center—they might look like an unassuming meeting or a routine project. But those who know the game understand the hidden value of these spaces.

For example, cross-departmental projects, low-profile yet highly visible meetings, or invitations to present your work can all be "power squares." They offer opportunities to establish a reputation quietly while building a foundation that others may not see coming. Recognizing these squares means positioning yourself strategically in areas that align with corporate objectives and give you access to key decision-makers. This is where your quiet moves can have an outsized impact.

Rule Insights

Rule 1: Nobody talks about playing the game. The unspoken rules of influence mean that power isn't always where it appears to be. Recognizing power squares within your organization allows you to navigate innocuously, placing yourself in critical roles where you can build influence without necessarily standing in the spotlight.

Strategy for Success

Not every opportunity on the board comes with a spotlight—some of the most valuable moves are hidden in plain sight, in spaces that only the discerning recognizes as strategic.

- ✓ Recognize influential spaces: Look for low-profile projects, committees, or meetings that have strategic value.
- ✓ Position strategically: Align yourself with these "power squares" to build influence without drawing unnecessary attention.
- ✓ Engage intentionally: Volunteer for cross-departmental initiatives or other roles that allow you to showcase your strengths to key decision-makers.

Identifying and leveraging power squares is about playing the long game — choosing roles and opportunities that amplify your strengths and align you with decision-makers. Quietly impactful moves on these squares can leave an out-sized impression, positioning you for lasting influence.

The Power of Adaptability

In chess, the board's landscape changes with every move. Each decision, each shift of a piece, creates a new set of possibilities and potential threats. Success in corporate spaces often requires the same adaptability: being able to reposition yourself when roles shift, departments restructure, or company priorities change. True adaptability means reading the board carefully, responding to each change with intention, and ensuring your moves align with your long-term strategy.

In one role, a sudden restructuring left many colleagues struggling to find their footing. By regularly reassessing my position, I could pivot quickly, identifying a new role that matched my strengths and goals. This adaptability protected my trajectory, positioning me as a dependable presence in times of uncertainty.

Remaining nimble prevents you from getting bogged down when the board shifts. It's not about constantly moving — it's about moving with purpose. Just as each piece on a chessboard must be ready to adapt to its changing landscape, staying flexible in your career helps you respond proactively rather than reactively, always one step ahead.

Rule Insights

Rule 5: Goalpost's gonna keep shifting. In corporate America, the expectations and priorities often shift without warning, and adaptability is your best defense. By staying nimble, you're prepared to pivot when goals change, or new demands arise, using each shift as an opportunity to reinforce your value. This adaptability isn't about reacting to every change; it's about anticipating and positioning yourself where you can have the most impact, even when the standards keep moving.

Strategy for Success

Success isn't about controlling the board — it's about being nimble enough to adjust to the moves others make while keeping your end game in sight.

- ✓ Reassess regularly: Periodically evaluate your role, strengths, and alignment with organizational priorities.
- ✓ Anticipate changes: Stay informed about potential shifts, such as departmental restructures or leadership transitions.
- ✓ Pivot with purpose: When changes occur, adjust your strategy to align with areas of growth or stability.
- ✓ Leverage shifts: Use organizational changes as opportunities to demonstrate your adaptability and value.

Adaptability ensures you're never caught off guard, always ready to turn shifts into stepping stones. By staying flexible and thinking, you create opportunities to thrive in uncertainty, proving your resilience and value in a constantly changing environment.

Observe Without Absorbing

The hardest part of studying the board is learning to observe without absorbing. Corporate dynamics can get messy, and it's easy to let them affect your confidence or self-worth. Observing means understanding the landscape without letting it define you.

Once, a colleague discreetly undermined my work, casting doubt on my contributions in ways I couldn't counter directly. It would have been easy to take their actions personally, but I learned to see their behavior as a reflection of their insecurities, not my worth. This boundary allowed me to stay grounded and focused on my path rather than someone else's insecurities.

Observing with detachment keeps you resilient and focused on your goals rather than getting sidetracked by someone else's agenda.

Rule Insights

Rule 1: Nobody talks about playing the game. Setting emotional boundaries ensures you remain focused in a game where motives aren't always transparent. Observing without absorbing allows you to assess the landscape while keeping your self-worth intact, aligning your path with your values rather than someone else's agenda.

Strategy for Success

In corporate spaces, where agendas and personalities clash, stepping back and observing without taking things personally is one of the most powerful tools you can wield.

- ✓ Set emotional boundaries: Understand workplace dynamics without letting them impact your confidence or self-worth.
- ✓ Detach from negativity: Recognize that others' behavior often reflects their insecurities, not your value.
- ✓ Stay focused: Focus on your goals and values, avoiding unnecessary distractions.

✓ Assess objectively: Use your observations to inform your strategy without internalizing biases or stress.

Mastering detachment allows you to navigate dynamics with clarity and focus, turning challenges into insights and setbacks into strategies. By maintaining emotional boundaries, you stay true to your path, grounded in your worth, and immune to the distractions of others' insecurities.

Key Takeaways

❖ Observe the Landscape: Take the time to understand the organizational layout, informal power structures, and unspoken dynamics before making your moves.

❖ Prioritize Strategic Positioning Over Visibility: Being seen doesn't always mean being valued. Choose roles and projects that align with your long-term goals and put you in a position of influence without necessarily taking center stage.

❖ Anticipate Shifts: Stay attuned to changes in company priorities, leadership, and industry trends. Being proactive about these shifts keeps you adaptable and ready for the next opportunity.

Food for Thought

❖ **Reflect:** Think about your workplace's last major shift or reorganization. How did people respond? Who adapted quickly, and who struggled to find their place?

❖ **Challenge:** Pick one team meeting this week to attend with the sole focus of observation. Watch how team members interact, who speaks up, and who holds silent authority. How does this impact your view of the dynamics in your organization?

Chapter 4: Guard Your Crown

In chess, the queen is the most powerful piece on the board — versatile, strong, and central to every strategy. But that strength comes with a catch: she's also a target. In corporate America, your "queen" is the essence of who you are — your unique strengths, skills, mental well-being, and your core identity. Guarding your crown means protecting these internal assets. While they are often what gives you an edge over others, they're also under constant scrutiny in professional spaces, especially for Black women. Guarding your crown is the key to your survival in the game.

Protecting Core Talents and Skills

In chess, the queen's expansive movement across the board gives her unparalleled power, but it also makes her a target. Similarly, your unique talents and skills serve as both the foundation of your success and a potential source of vulnerability. In corporate spaces, these strengths often become the currency of advancement—but only if you actively protect and leverage them.

For Black women, navigating this dynamic comes with unique challenges. Talents that might be celebrated when displayed by others are often undervalued or dismissed, leaving you to work twice as hard for half the recognition. Worse still, these strengths can be co-opted by colleagues who are quick to claim credit while leaving you out of the spotlight. Safeguarding your skills isn't just about recognizing your value; it's also about maintaining control over your narrative and ensuring that your contributions are unmistakably yours.

To thrive, you must recognize that the power of your talents lies in their visibility and alignment with your career goals. When your unique abilities are showcased strategically, they become tools for creating influence, building allies, and carving a path that reflects your strengths. Without proactive measures, your talents risk becoming invisible or diluted by the demands of a workplace that doesn't always reward innovation or excellence equally.

Early in my career, I developed a reporting system that boosted efficiency across the team. But rather than celebrating my contribution, it was quietly absorbed into the routine, almost blending into the background. The turning point came when I saw my work featured in a presentation, credited to the team rather than me. From that moment, I knew I had to establish my narrative. I made it a habit to document my progress and share results with key stakeholders. Each milestone became a moment to reinforce my role, and this self-advocacy not only highlighted my contributions but shifted perceptions, showing that my skills were essential, not disposable.

Rule Insights

Rule 3: Their best is your mediocre. For us, consistently excellent work is often seen as the bare minimum. Guarding your talents means acknowledging them as unique assets rather than letting others take them for granted.

Strategy for Success

Safeguard your core talents and skills with these actionable steps:

- ✓ Document your contributions: Maintain a portfolio of your work, tracking key projects, accomplishments, and feedback. This ensures you have evidence of your impact if your contributions are questioned or minimized.
- ✓ Showcase your value: Regularly update colleagues and supervisors on your progress through presentations, email updates, or one-on-one check-ins. Don't assume your work will speak for itself — be the voice behind it.
- ✓ Align your skills with goals: Focus on projects that highlight your strengths and align with your career aspirations. This makes your talents visible to those who matter while ensuring your work contributes to your long-term trajectory.
- ✓ Set boundaries: Learn to say no to tasks or roles that don't align with your strengths or that risk

spreading you too thin. Guarding your energy is part of protecting your talents.

✓ Build your brand: Use platforms like LinkedIn or internal company networks to establish a reputation for excellence in your expertise. Sharing your insights or achievements increases your visibility and reinforces your value.

Your talents and skills are your most reliable allies in the corporate game, but their value depends on your ability to protect, nurture, and showcase them. By being deliberate about how you leverage your strengths, you ensure that your contributions are not only recognized but also respected. The path to success is not about playing small to fit in; it is about standing tall and ensuring your brilliance is undeniable.

Prioritizing Mental Health

In chess, the queen serves as a stabilizing force, anchoring the board even in moments of uncertainty. Mental well-being plays a similar role in life and work: it's the foundation of your strength and the key to navigating challenges with clarity and intention. For Black women in corporate spaces, the expectation of endless resilience often leaves little room to acknowledge—or tend to—the toll that stress takes.

The unspoken expectation to always be "strong" creates a cycle in which Black women are seen as capable but not vulnerable, celebrated for their work ethic but overlooked when it comes to the need for rest. This dynamic can erode mental well-being over time, leading to burnout, reduced focus, and even physical health challenges. Prioritizing mental health isn't a luxury, it's a necessity for maintaining excellence in professional spaces.

Learning to prioritize your mental health starts with recognizing its value. It's about understanding that recharging isn't selfish; it's an investment in your long-term success. Just as the queen on the chessboard is strategically protected to maintain the game's balance, safeguarding your mental well-being ensures you have the energy, focus, and clarity to continue making impactful moves.

In one role, balancing heavy workloads and constant feedback loops started to wear on me. I hit a point where I had to prioritize my mental well-being. So, I set "offline" times and blocked periods in my calendar for uninterrupted work. Initially, enforcing these blocks felt almost defiant, but it was a necessary shift for my long-term mental health. Over time, these boundaries preserved my peace of mind and sustained my performance. Prioritizing my mental health wasn't just about staying afloat; it was about protecting my ability to keep delivering excellence.

Rule Insights

Rule 5: Goalpost's gonna keep shifting. The constant demand for excellence can push Black women to overextend themselves in environments with ever-changing expectations. Setting boundaries and prioritizing mental health helps you stay steady in a game designed to keep you off balance.

Rule 7: Ain't nobody coming to save you. Corporate initiatives on mental health are often performative, making it essential for you to prioritize self-care independently. Guarding your mental health is about protecting your ability to thrive in the long run. Think marathon, not sprint.

Strategy for Success

Protect your mental well-being with deliberate and actionable steps:

- ✓ Set Non-Negotiable Boundaries: Establish precise work hours, create "offline" times, and block out your calendar for uninterrupted work or personal recharge periods. Communicate these boundaries clearly and unapologetically.
- ✓ Create Recovery Rituals: Incorporate regular practices like journaling, meditation, therapy, or fitness into your routine to decompress and manage stress. These rituals are essential tools for preserving your peace of mind.
- ✓ Say No Strategically: Avoid overloading your plate by declining

tasks or roles that don't align with your goals or unnecessarily drain your energy. Saying no is a form of self-care.

✓ Leverage Your Support Network: Build and maintain relationships with colleagues, mentors, or friends who encourage your well-being. A trusted network can provide perspective and help you navigate challenges.

✓ Advocate for Yourself: When workloads become unmanageable, or expectations feel unreasonable, advocate for additional resources or adjustments. Self-advocacy is critical to maintaining balance and mental health.

✓ Recognize the Warning Signs: Pay attention to the physical and emotional signals of burnout, such as chronic fatigue, irritability, or difficulty focusing. Acting early prevents minor issues from escalating into crises.

Prioritizing mental health is an act of strength, not weakness. It allows you to bring your whole self to the table—

focused, energized, and capable of making impactful moves. Protecting your peace of mind isn't about stepping away from the game but ensuring you remain a powerful presence on the board. By setting boundaries and advocating for your well-being, you reinforce your values and sustain your brilliance for the long run.

Embracing Your Presence and Power

On the chessboard, the queen's presence commands respect, influencing every move, even when not in action. In the workplace, your self-worth and identity play a similar role, anchoring your resilience and confidence amidst the challenges of bias, dismissal, or underestimation. Yet, navigating spaces that fail to recognize your contributions can test that inner strength and challenge your sense of belonging.

For Black women in corporate spaces, the demand to constantly prove their value can make it difficult to separate their self-worth from external validation. When recognition is uneven—or outright absent—redefining success on your terms is essential. Embracing your power means understanding that your value is not contingent on others' acknowledgment but on your work's authenticity, integrity, and impact. Just as the queen on the board remains the most powerful piece regardless of how others perceive her, you must operate with the quiet confidence that your presence alone carries weight.

Finding and holding onto that confidence begins with reframing how you measure your worth. It's not about who claps for you, echoes your ideas, or gives you credit. Instead, it's about knowing that your contributions matter, documenting your impact, and consistently showing up as your best self. When you center your self-worth internally, external perceptions lose power over you.

I noticed a pattern in one organization: my ideas were acknowledged only when someone else repeated them. At first, this was disheartening, but it taught me to separate my worth from their recognition. After witnessing my ideas gain

171

traction only when parroted by others, I realized I had to set my own metrics for success and track them. I began documenting my contributions, voicing my thoughts confidently, and creating benchmarks for success. My self-worth no longer depended on others' approval but on the integrity and impact of my work.

Strategy for Success

Building self-worth and confidence in the workplace requires proactive strategies:

- ✓ Create Your Own Metrics: Set personal benchmarks for success based on the quality and impact of your work, not just external validation. Track your contributions to remind yourself of your accomplishments.
- ✓ Document Everything: Maintain a detailed record of your ideas, projects, and outcomes. This will reinforce your confidence and ensure you have evidence to back up your value when needed.

✓ Voice Your Ideas With Confidence: Speak up with authority, even if recognition doesn't come immediately. Consistency in your delivery builds credibility over time.

✓ Define Your Value Independently: Reflect on your strengths and contributions outside of work. Whether through personal projects, community involvement, or creative outlets, find ways to reaffirm your worth beyond your job title.

✓ Celebrate Your Wins: Big or small, take time to acknowledge and celebrate your successes. Internal validation strengthens your ability to navigate spaces that fail to recognize your value.

✓ Build a Support Network: Surround yourself with people who see and affirm your worth. Trusted allies can provide perspective, encouragement, and advocacy when you need it most.

✓ Let Recognition Find You: Focus on doing the work that aligns with your values and goals. Recognition will follow, but don't make it your sole pursuit.

Embracing your presence and power begins with understanding that your worth isn't contingent on others' opinions or acknowledgment. Like the queen on the chessboard, your value is intrinsic and undeniable, shaping the game simply by being there. By defining your own metrics for success, advocating for yourself, and celebrating your wins, you reclaim your power and ensure that no one else controls the narrative of your worth.

Rule Insights

Rule 1: Nobody talks about playing the game. We must set our own standards in spaces where our worth might not be openly acknowledged. By defining our value internally, we refuse to let others diminish our presence or contributions.

Rule 3: Their best is your mediocre. For Black women, excellence is often the baseline, not the celebrated exception. By embracing your power and redefining success on your terms, you prevent external biases from undermining your confidence or diminishing your contributions.

Preserving Self Without Sacrifice

On the board, Black women are often celebrated for their strength and resilience, but this expectation can come at a significant cost. True resilience doesn't mean enduring endless pressure or powering through adversity to the point of exhaustion. Instead, it's about balancing strength with self-preservation, maintaining your well-being, values, and boundaries even in environments that may push you to your limits.

Resilience rooted in self-preservation is a reclamation of power. It means knowing when to say no, stepping back when the cost to your mental or physical health becomes too high, and unapologetically protecting your peace. Resilience without self-awareness often leads to burnout, but when coupled with boundaries, it becomes a sustainable force that allows you to thrive over the long term.

In one role, I took pride in "powering through" everything, regardless of the toll. But after a grueling week that left me questioning my health and performance, I realized that resilience shouldn't mean endless endurance. I shifted my definition of resilience to setting boundaries, taking breaks, and respecting my limits. This shift allowed me to keep performing well while also safeguarding my well-being. I learned that true resilience is about caring for myself in a way that sustains my ability to thrive.

This shift can feel counterintuitive. The pressure to prove our worth often makes us overextend ourselves, taking pride in enduring what others might not even notice. However, strength without sustainability is a recipe for depletion and disaster. Preserving yourself while navigating corporate spaces is not a sign of weakness but an act of self-respect and a strategy for long-term success.

Strategy for Success

Resilience is not about enduring everything but preserving yourself while remaining effective. Here are practical ways to balance strength and self-care:

- ✓ Set Boundaries: Be intentional about where you draw the line. Whether it's blocking off time for focused work, declining unnecessary meetings, or saying no to extra responsibilities, boundaries are essential to preserving your well-being.
- ✓ Redefine Resilience: Strength includes knowing when to rest, step back, or recalibrate. Resilience isn't about enduring; it's about thriving without compromising your health or values.
- ✓ Prioritize Rest and Recovery: Schedule regular breaks throughout your day and treat downtime as non-negotiable. Rest is not a luxury—it's a necessity for sustained performance.
- ✓ Be Selective About Your Energy: Identify which tasks, projects, or people align with your goals and values, and focus your energy there. Not every battle is worth fighting.

- ✓ Advocate for Yourself: If your workload becomes unreasonable, communicate your limits clearly and professionally. Proactive advocacy ensures your needs are heard while maintaining your credibility.
- ✓ Check in With Yourself Regularly: Reflect on how you feel mentally, emotionally, and physically. If you notice signs of burnout or fatigue, adjust your approach immediately.
- ✓ Enlist Allies: Build a support system at work and outside. Trusted allies can help ease your load, offer perspective, and reinforce your boundaries.
- ✓ Celebrate Saying No: Recognize that turning down an opportunity or declining extra work isn't failure — it's a strategic choice to protect your capacity and deliver where it matters most.

Preserving yourself while navigating corporate spaces isn't about doing less; it's about doing what matters most without sacrificing your well-being or identity. True resilience is rooted in self-awareness and self-respect, ensuring that your strength remains sustainable over the long term. You reclaim the power to thrive on your terms by redefining resilience and setting boundaries.

Rule Insights

Rule 5: Goalpost's gonna keep shifting. On the board, demands are rarely static. Resilience is as much about self-care as it is about strength, ensuring that we're prepared for an environment where boundaries are constantly tested.

Honoring Your Narrative

The queen commands respect through her presence, strategy, and integrity. In the workplace, embracing transparency is a powerful way to assert your narrative and maintain your integrity. You create an authentic and respected professional identity by clarifying your values, boundaries, and expectations. Transparency allows you to set the tone for how you operate, making your intentions and priorities clear while establishing a reputation rooted in honesty and respect.

I quickly realized that vague language and half-hearted agreements were the cultural norm in one organization. Colleagues often sidestepped directness, and unclear commitments frequently derailed projects. Rather than adopting this approach, I embraced transparency and directness during team discussions and one-on-one meetings. Though initially uncomfortable in a culture that seemed to reward ambiguity, this approach slowly set me apart. Over time, my openness earned the respect of my colleagues, positioning me as someone who valued clarity and authenticity. This grounded my professional relationships and influenced how others engaged with me, fostering a stronger culture of respect and collaboration. That said, mileage varies. Company culture dictates how direct you can be with colleagues and peers, so when in doubt, see Chapter Three for tips on adapting to varying dynamics.

Honoring your narrative doesn't mean over-sharing or being transparent to a fault; it means setting clear boundaries and expectations while staying true to your values. This can be particularly important for Black women navigating corporate spaces, as transparency can help dismantle stereotypes and encourage others to engage with you on your terms. However, it also requires strategic discernment—choosing when and how to share to align with your goals while protecting your energy.

Strategy for Success

Transparency is a skill that requires both self-awareness and strategy. Here are ways to honor your narrative while fostering trust and respect:

- ✓ Clarify Your Boundaries: Be explicit about what you need to succeed—uninterrupted work time, clear deadlines, or specific support. Transparency about your boundaries helps prevent misunderstandings and sets the stage for collaboration.
- ✓ Be Direct Yet Diplomatic: Approach conversations with clarity but remain tactful, especially in environments where directness may be misinterpreted. Transparency doesn't have to mean

bluntness; it's about being clear while maintaining professionalism.

✓ Establish Consistency: Align your actions with your words to reinforce authenticity. When others see that your transparency is consistent and genuine, it builds trust and respect.

✓ Practice Strategic Sharing: Transparency doesn't mean revealing everything. Share enough to clarify your values and expectations but protect personal details or vulnerabilities that may not serve your goals.

✓ Tailor Your Approach to the Culture: Observe the corporate culture to gauge the appropriate level of transparency. In more formal or hierarchical environments, subtle transparency—like setting clear meeting goals—may be more effective than outright directness.

✓ Document Your Contributions: Transparency in your work ensures your efforts are recognized. Share updates, provide summaries of your achievements, and establish a clear record of your impact.

✓ Lead by Example: Transparency is contagious. By modeling clear communication, you encourage others to adopt similar practices, fostering a more open and collaborative environment.

Honoring your narrative through transparency is a commitment to authenticity and self-respect. While it may require navigating cultural nuances or overcoming discomfort, it sets a foundation for meaningful engagement and professional growth. By embracing transparency strategically, you establish your value and inspire others to meet you with the same clarity and integrity.

Rule Insights

Rule 1: Nobody talks about playing the game. Transparency can challenge the unspoken rules of corporate spaces, where ambiguity often governs interactions. By openly defining your values and boundaries, you create clarity in environments that thrive on hidden expectations, positioning yourself as someone who operates with integrity and confidence.

Rule 5: Goalpost's gonna keep shifting. In workplaces where expectations frequently change, being clear about who you are and what you stand for helps you navigate shifting priorities without losing sight of your purpose. Transparency is an anchor, allowing you to stay grounded even as the game rules evolve.

Guarding Your Crown With Purpose

Guarding your crown means honoring and protecting the core of who you are, your strengths, well-being, self-worth, and your very essence. It's about navigating challenges without letting them define you and maintaining your strength, integrity, and identity regardless of what comes your way. Black women, in particular, often bear the weight of both expectation and scrutiny, which makes protecting your crown even more critical. It's not just about defense; it's about standing firm in your worth and using every experience to strengthen your resolve.

Imagine you're in a role where your ideas are frequently co-opted by a more senior colleague, who frames them as their own in meetings. Rather than allowing this behavior to undermine your confidence or define your contributions, guarding your crown could mean documenting your ideas in emails to relevant stakeholders or presenting your ideas directly when the opportunity arises. You protect your work by maintaining clear communication and ensuring your voice is heard without allowing someone else's actions to dictate your worth or trajectory. In this case, guarding your crown is about leveraging strategy to preserve your value and visibility, no matter the circumstances.

Rule Insights

Rule 3: Their best is your mediocre. For Black women, excellence is often seen as the minimum, making it crucial to protect your contributions and ensure they are recognized. Guarding your crown means documenting your ideas and achievements, asserting your value, and ensuring that others do not diminish or co-opt your efforts.

Rule 4: There can only be one. Corporate spaces often pit Black women against each other or frame success as a zero-sum game. Guarding your crown helps you resist these divisive narratives by staying focused on your unique strengths and refusing to let external pressures diminish your self-worth or push you into unnecessary competition.

Rule 6: Shade is inevitable. Navigating the workplace comes with inevitable moments of bias, microaggressions, or outright undermining. Guarding your crown ensures that such negativity doesn't define you or derail your progress. Instead, you proactively protect your peace and leverage strategic actions to ensure your value remains visible and intact.

Strategy for Success

Guarding your crown begins with understanding your intrinsic value and ensuring it remains intact despite external challenges. It's about staying true to your identity, principles, and well-being while navigating the complexities of the workplace. A proactive approach will allow you to thrive without compromising the essence of who you are.

- ✓ Regularly assess your priorities. Identify areas where you feel stretched too thin or undervalued and adjust accordingly.
- ✓ Set boundaries. Protect your mental, emotional, and physical well-being by learning when to say no, delegate, or request support.
- ✓ Advocate for your contributions. Document your achievements and ensure they are visible to the right stakeholders.
- ✓ Adapt your strategies. Reassess what "guarding your crown" means at different stages of your career and adjust as necessary to maintain balance and fulfillment.

✓ Build and nurture a support network. Surround yourself with trusted allies who celebrate your strengths and support your boundaries.

Ultimately, guarding your crown is not about resisting every challenge but ensuring you emerge from them stronger, wiser, and unwavering in your self-worth. Maintaining this focus creates a foundation for long-term growth and fulfillment that honors your professional and personal aspirations.

Key Takeaways

❖ Protect Your Unique Talents: Your skills and contributions are your assets. Proactively ensure your contributions are recognized as assets that cannot be minimized or overlooked.

❖ Prioritize Mental Health as Strength: Resilience doesn't mean enduring everything without pause. Your peace and mental clarity are essential, not optional.

❖ Define Your Self-Worth: Your value is inherent and not tied to others' perceptions. Establish your own standards of success and hold on to them.

Food for Thought

❖ **Reflect:** Think of a time when you felt undervalued at work. What could have been different if you had stronger boundaries around your time, skills, or self-worth?

❖ **Challenge:** Identify one area where you've been giving too much of yourself. Take a small but concrete action this week to create or reinforce a boundary there and note how it makes you feel.

Nicole S. Palmer

Chapter 5: Protect Your Rep

The queen may command the board in chess, but the king determines survival. Lose the king, and the game's over. On the board, your "king" is your reputation—your "rep." It's the asset that shapes how others perceive your skills, character, and competence. And let's be honest: for Black women, our reputation comes under extra scrutiny. Where others get the benefit of the doubt, we're often expected to prove ourselves over and over. Guarding this reputation isn't just a matter of career strategy; it's about fortifying our standing, so setbacks don't define our future.

This chapter will discuss strategies to defend your reputation with the same vigilance a grandmaster guards the king. And, if you're wondering, a grandmaster is the highest title you can be awarded in chess (aside from World Champion, but you're not here for that). You'll ensure that your rep stays resilient by managing your image, handling stereotypes, and knowing when to step into the spotlight.

Building a Foundation

A solid defense around the king is essential to long-term survival and victory in chess. Similarly, in the workplace, your reputation serves as your foundation, a shield fortified through the quality of your work, your interactions, and your ability to deliver consistently. For Black women, the stakes are often higher, as our reputations are scrutinized more harshly and frequently underestimated. Intentionality is the key to building a solid foundation: treating every task, no matter how small, as an opportunity to showcase your value and reliability.

In one of my earlier roles, I worked for someone notably hard to please. The department needed clearer documentation practices, leaving much room for misunderstandings and misrepresentation. Unfortunately, this manager would shift blame quickly, often painting me as the issue. Without documentation, it became my word against theirs, and I found myself at a disadvantage. That experience taught me the value of meticulously documenting my work and interactions. Now, I keep track of every project, every milestone, and every bit of feedback, good or bad. Over time, this habit has helped ensure that my reputation is backed by facts, protecting it from biases and misinterpretations.

Rule Insights

Rule 3: Their best is your mediocre. For Black women, consistently excellent work is often seen as "doing our job." Guarding your rep means recognizing your strengths and protecting against the assumption that your excellence is merely a baseline.

Rule 7: Ain't nobody coming to save you. Protecting your reputation is a proactive act in environments where credit is not freely given. Your foundation becomes a safeguard when others fail to acknowledge your efforts.

Strategy for Success

A strong foundation is built one brick at a time through intentional actions and consistent quality. Whether you're working on a high-stakes project or handling routine tasks, approach each with the same level of diligence to protect and enhance your professional reputation.

- ✓ Document your work meticulously. Keep a record of deliverables, milestones, and feedback to ensure your contributions are clear and verifiable.
- ✓ Prioritize quality in every task. Treat small, unnoticed tasks with the same commitment as high-visibility ones.
- ✓ Clarify expectations early. Confirm goals, deadlines, and roles to eliminate ambiguity and ensure measurable success.
- ✓ Proactively share progress. Regularly update key stakeholders to maintain transparency and ownership of your work.
- ✓ Address missteps openly. If issues arise, take accountability while clearly outlining solutions, reinforcing your reliability.

A strong foundation doesn't just protect you—it propels you. By treating every interaction and deliverable as an opportunity to build trust and demonstrate excellence, you create a reputation that defends you and opens doors to new opportunities.

Shielding Against Misperceptions

Navigating stereotypes and biases in the workplace can feel like walking a tightrope, especially when dealing with labels like the "Angry Black Woman." This harmful stereotype can turn assertiveness into hostility in the eyes of others, creating barriers that distort how our contributions and professionalism are perceived. For Black women, the challenge is often twofold: advocating for ourselves while maintaining an image that doesn't trigger these biases. It's a frustrating and exhausting balancing act but can be approached with strategy and intentionality.

Imagine being assigned a critical project but finding additional responsibilities quietly shifted into your lap, far beyond your initial scope. Recognizing the potential for burnout, you raise the issue with your manager, framing your concerns as a way to ensure the team's success rather than as a critique of the workload. Despite your thoughtful phrasing, whispers begin circulating about you being "difficult" or "not a team player." Balancing professionalism with self-advocacy becomes a delicate but essential skill in such scenarios.

At the same time, there's an important caveat: no strategy will work in every environment. Toxic workplaces, riddled with systemic bias and deep-seated "-isms," may not allow for successful navigation of misperceptions, no matter how carefully you communicate. In such cases, the best action is to protect your peace by finding an environment where your value is recognized and respected.

Rule Insights

Rule 1: Nobody talks about playing the game. Navigating stereotypes requires care in spaces where people may judge without fully understanding. It's about striking a balance, conveying the strength of your presence while keeping the focus on your professionalism.

Rule 5: Goalpost's gonna keep shifting. The standards of professionalism can feel like a moving target, especially for Black women. By proactively managing how your actions are perceived, you can navigate these shifting expectations while staying true to your values.

Rule 7: Ain't nobody coming to save you. Misperceptions thrive in silence. Advocating for yourself and addressing biases head-on ensures that your reputation reflects your contributions, even when others attempt to distort them.

Strategy for Success

Protecting against misperceptions requires intentional communication, professionalism, and advocating for yourself. While this approach won't work in every environment, it can create opportunities to shift perceptions in spaces where change is possible.

- ✓ Phrase your concerns strategically. When addressing challenges, frame them as collaborative and solution-focused rather than confrontational.

- ✓ Document conversations and actions. Keep records of discussions, decisions, and deliverables to counter any misrepresentation of your role or behavior.
- ✓ Seek allies and advocates. Build relationships with colleagues and mentors who can support your contributions and advocate on your behalf when needed.
- ✓ Redirect narratives. If you hear damaging whispers, address them subtly by reinforcing your professionalism and commitment in future interactions.
- ✓ Know when to walk away. If biases are too entrenched, focus on finding a healthier work environment where your worth is acknowledged.

Shielding your reputation isn't about appeasing others, it's about protecting the integrity of your work and maintaining your sense of self in spaces that may challenge it. By advocating for yourself with intention and knowing when to exit toxic situations, you preserve your ability to thrive on your terms.

Managing Perception

In chess, the king's position determines his influence, often shaped by the protective strategies of surrounding pieces. In the workplace, your influence operates similarly: how you're perceived often shapes your opportunities and challenges. For Black women, perception management becomes even more nuanced, as biases and stereotypes can unfairly influence how professionalism and competence are judged.

The workplace often imposes narrow definitions of what is considered "professional." From communication style to physical presentation, these standards can feel like a tightrope act for Black women. Something as simple as a hairstyle can become a battleground for perception, with natural or cultural styles sometimes interpreted as less "polished." Managing perception is less about changing who you are and more about ensuring that your authenticity and professionalism remain visible and aligned with your goals.

I often received different responses based on how I wore my hair. With my locs styled in a sleek bun, I'd receive compliments and more positive attention from colleagues, but when worn naturally, reactions were notably quieter. Over time, I realized that their responses were rooted in biases, not in my professionalism. Now, I choose styles that make me feel confident, grounding my self-worth in my competence rather than their perceptions. Managing perception isn't about conforming; it's about being intentional in what you project while staying true to yourself.

Rule Insights

Rule 3: Their best is your mediocre. Managing perception ensures that your excellence is recognized. By aligning your actions and presentation with your expertise, you remind others that your competence isn't conditional, it's inherent.

Rule 7: Ain't nobody coming to save you. Managing perception is your responsibility in environments where biases and assumptions run deep. By strategically positioning yourself, you protect your reputation from misinterpretations and establish value on your terms.

Strategy for Success

When it comes to managing perception, think of it as curating your brand:

- ✓ Pay attention to first impressions: High-stakes situations, like interviews or leadership presentations, often shape how others perceive you long-term. Prepare intentionally to leave a lasting, positive impact.

- ✓ Communicate with precision and authenticity: Ensure your words reflect your expertise and values when speaking. Active listening and thoughtful responses often leave a stronger impression than overexplaining or trying to adapt to others' expectations.

- ✓ Challenge biases subtly: When possible, correct misperceptions in a professional, calm manner. For example, if someone misinterprets your tone, reframe the conversation to refocus on the substance of your message.

✓ Own your narrative: Define your professional image by consistently demonstrating excellence and aligning your actions with your long-term goals.

Managing perception is not about conforming to every expectation but balancing authenticity with intentionality. By being mindful of the image you project, you can shape how others perceive you without compromising who you are.

Highlighting Without Alienating

In corporate spaces, success is a double-edged sword. While your achievements can set you apart, they can also attract unnecessary scrutiny or resentment, particularly for Black women navigating workplaces where recognition may be uneven. Success often brings the additional challenge of balancing confidence with humility, demonstrating your impact without overshadowing others or inviting misinterpretation.

We are often held to different standards when celebrating our wins. The line between being seen as confident and labeled "arrogant" can be thin. High-lighting your achievements doesn't mean hiding your light; it means manag-ing the narrative around your contribu-tions in a way that reinforces your lead-ership while fostering collaboration.

Imagine leading a team through a chal-lenging product launch where tight deadlines and shifting requirements sometimes made success feel impossible. After delivering on time and exceeding key performance metrics, you present the results during a department-wide meeting. Instead of simply stating that you led the project, you highlight how collaboration made success possible: ."This project taught me a lot about man-aging under pressure, but it wouldn't have been possible without the team's adaptability and problem-solving. We met the deadline and exceeded the ex-pected revenue target by 15%. I'm in-credibly proud of our accomplishments and grateful for everyone's hard work."

This approach achieves two key objec-tives. First, it showcases your leadership in steering the team through adversity.

Second, it reinforces your role as a collab-orative, inclusive leader, positioning you as someone who uplifts others while achieving results.

Rule Insights

Rule 3: Their best is your mediocre. Black women often face heightened scrutiny in how they celebrate achievements. By framing your wins with humility and context, you ensure your excellence is visible and undeniable rather than misin-terpreted as overconfidence.

Rule 4: There can only be one. In spaces where your success might be perceived as competition, positioning your wins as part of a more significant effort makes your contributions stand out while keep-ing relationships intact. Success becomes something to build on rather than some-thing that separates.

Strategy for Success

When highlighting your achievements, consider these steps to strike the right balance:

- ✓ Anchor your wins in the team's success: Share the spotlight by recognizing your team's contributions and emphasizing collective effort. This approach builds goodwill while subtly reinforcing your role as a leader.

✓ Be intentional with your timing: Highlight achievements in contexts where your audience can appreciate their significance, such as during team meetings or performance reviews.

✓ Use data to support your claims: Present results objectively using metrics or tangible outcomes to show your impact without sounding overly self-congratulatory.

✓ Celebrate learning: Frame your achievements as part of a broader growth journey, showing humility and a willingness to continue improving.

✓ Show gratitude: Express appreciation for others' support, whether colleagues, mentors, or team members, to create an atmosphere of shared success.

Balancing visibility with collaboration isn't about minimizing your role but

ensuring your contributions are celebrated without alienating others. By
highlighting your achievements with intention and inclusivity, you position
yourself as a confident, capable leader
while reinforcing the value of teamwork.

Tracking the King's Moves

In chess, remembering the King's moves
allows you to anticipate threats and plan
your defenses effectively. Similarly,
keeping track of your achievements, critical conversations, and feedback is essential in your career. For Black women, this
isn't just about self-promotion; it's about
ensuring that your contributions are documented and undeniable. Without a
clear record, even significant successes
can be overlooked or questioned, leaving
you vulnerable to misrepresentation or
bias.

Maintaining documentation becomes especially critical when dealing with performance reviews, sudden shifts in priorities, or challenging conversations with
leadership. It's not just about defending
your reputation; it's about ensuring your
career trajectory remains based on your

contributions, not someone else's mis-characterization.

Imagine you've been managing a critical project for months, hitting every milestone and exceeding expectations. Then, during a quarterly review, your manager downplays your role, attributing much of the success to "the team" while ignoring your leadership. If you've been tracking your work—recording metrics, saving emails with positive feedback, and documenting milestones—you can confidently present your impact, leaving no room for debate about your contributions.

Rule Insights

Rule 5: Goalpost's gonna keep shifting. In environments where recognition can be inconsistent, having a record of your achievements helps protect your reputation. It's a safeguard against corporate America's shifting standards and evolving demands.

Rule 7: Ain't nobody coming to save you. Relying solely on others to advocate for your value is a risk. Keeping records ensures you can advocate for yourself and protect your career when others fall short.

Strategy for Success

When it comes to documenting your contributions and progress, consider these steps:

- ✓ Maintain an achievement portfolio: Track metrics, deliverables, and successful outcomes from your work. Include specific numbers or results wherever possible to provide concrete evidence of your impact.
- ✓ Record key conversations: After meetings or performance discussions, summarize key takeaways and send a follow-up email to confirm agreements. This paper trail can clarify expectations and protect you from misrepresentation.
- ✓ Save positive feedback: Create a folder for emails, comments, or reviews highlighting your strengths. These are valuable for

performance reviews or advocating for promotions.

✓ Log challenges and resolutions: Document instances where you faced obstacles but found solutions. These examples demonstrate your ability to adapt and excel under pressure.

✓ Stay consistent: Make documentation a habit, not a one-time effort. Regularly updating your records ensures that you're always prepared.

Having a well-maintained record isn't just about defending your reputation; it's a tool for showcasing your growth and advocating for your value. By tracking your career moves with the precision of a seasoned chess player, you ensure that your narrative remains clear, accurate, and firmly in your control. We must always be above reproach. Having years, even decades of experience at a company can be wiped away in an instant if they even believe for a moment, you are displaying any of the ingrained stereotypes we battle against — the most common being the angry Black woman.

Safeguarding Your Career

Your reputation is the literal king on the board, which determines your long-term standing, even when the game gets tough. Guarding it requires vigilance, perception management, and a balance of humility and strength. Maintaining a reputation above reproach is critical in the corporate landscape, where Black women's achievements often undergo heightened scrutiny.

Consider a scenario where a colleague begins subtly undermining your contributions, planting seeds of doubt about your competence. Without a clear sense of your reputation and how it aligns with your goals, this behavior could spiral, damaging your professional standing. However, by remaining composed, consistently delivering excellence, and reinforcing your value through visible achievements and documented contributions, you protect your reputation and solidify it as a tool to counter such attempts.

Rule Insights

Rule 5: Goalpost's gonna keep shifting. Maintaining a solid and adaptable reputation helps shield you from unfair scrutiny in a constantly evolving landscape where expectations and standards evolve.

Rule 3: Their best is your mediocre. Guarding your reputation means ensuring your excellence is recognized for what it is—not just baseline performance.

Strategy for Success

When it comes to safeguarding your reputation, think strategically:

- ✓ Conduct regular self-assessments: Periodically evaluate your professional image to ensure it aligns with your long-term goals and values. Adjust as needed to stay on track.
- ✓ Own your narrative: Proactively communicate your achievements and impact to reflect your strengths and contributions. Don't let others define your story.

✓ Build a network of advocates: Cultivate relationships with trusted colleagues, mentors, or sponsors who can vouch for your integrity and accomplishments.

✓ Document your contributions: Keep detailed records of your achievements, feedback, and key interactions to ensure your reputation is supported by tangible evidence.

✓ Stay adaptable: Be willing to pivot your approach when needed, aligning your actions and visibility with changing expectations or challenges.

Guarding your reputation requires more than just managing external perceptions. It's about protecting your core values while navigating the complexities of corporate spaces. Treating your reputation as the King on the board ensures it remains a source of strength, resilience, and direction for your career.

Key Takeaways

❖ Build a reputation that speaks for itself: Every project, interaction, and choice add to your legacy. Let your work reflect the integrity and excellence you bring to every space.

❖ Counter stereotypes with precision: Recognize how others may misinterpret confidence or assertiveness. Strategically frame your actions to keep the focus on your professionalism and impact.

❖ Document your contributions: Keep records of your work and achievements. A solid paper trail reinforces your story, ensuring your impact is visible, undeniable, and can't be rewritten.

Food for Thought

❖ **Reflect:** How would you define the professional reputation you aspire to have? Consider qualities like reliability, integrity, and innovation.

❖ **Challenge:** This week, make it a point to highlight one of your

recent accomplishments in a subtle way that reinforces your reputation. It might be through a team
update, a progress report, or a
quick message to a supervisor.

Chapter 6: Take Center Stage

In chess, the queen's strength comes from her command of the board's center. From there, she influences the game, maximizing her impact and control. Taking center stage in corporate America isn't much different—it's about positioning yourself intentionally, so your contributions shine and your presence resonates. For Black women, though, "taking center stage" can come with risks: increased scrutiny, stereotypes, or even backlash. It's a delicate dance, one that requires strength and subtlety. In this chapter, we'll look at ways to take the center with purpose, ensuring your impact is undeniable while navigating the biases that may come your way.

Commanding the Center Without Apology

Just as the queen commands power from the center of the board, Black women must advocate for themselves in corporate spaces to ensure their contributions are recognized and respected. Self-advocacy can be a delicate balancing act, as perceptions of assertiveness are often unfairly tied to stereotypes. Yet, owning your accomplishments and positioning yourself strategically ensures that your work speaks for itself. This is not about seeking the spotlight but establishing undeniable influence and creating a foundation of visibility for your contributions.

Imagine leading a major initiative where your team achieves significant results, and the success hinges on your ability to organize resources and build consensus. After the project wraps, leadership recognizes the team's efforts but doesn't specifically mention your role in orchestrating the outcome. Instead of letting this oversight diminish your visibility, you prepare a concise summary of the project's impact and your contributions, which you share in a follow-up email to your manager and key stakeholders. This reinforces the results and positions you as a leader who understands the value of collaboration while ensuring your role is clear.

I handled a high-profile project early in my career, but my work was often credited to others in meetings. Frustrating? Of course, it was. So, I started summarizing key accomplishments and sending updates directly to my manager, linking my work to the team's broader objectives. This ensured my contributions stayed visible without needing to be on the floor every moment. Self-advocacy doesn't mean seeking the spotlight; it's about keeping your impact clear and undeniable.

Rule Insights

Rule 5: Goalpost's gonna keep shifting. In environments where the standards for recognition are inconsistent or unclear, proactive self-advocacy ensures your contributions are not overlooked or diminished.

Rule 7: Ain't nobody coming to save you. Waiting for others to recognize your value is a risk. You control how your work is perceived and credited by owning your narrative.

Strategy for Success

When it comes to commanding the center without apology, keep the following in mind:

- ✓ Position your achievements strategically: Frame your accomplishments in the context of team or organizational goals, tying your success to broader outcomes.
- ✓ Document your impact: Keep a running record of your contributions, feedback, and milestones to provide clarity when advocating for yourself.
- ✓ Communicate with intention: Share updates highlighting your contributions without diminishing others. This balance ensures your self-advocacy is viewed as professionalism, not arrogance.
- ✓ Seek visibility in high-impact spaces: Volunteer for cross-departmental projects or other initiatives that align with your strengths and give you exposure to key decision-makers.
- ✓ Leverage allies: Build a network of supporters who can amplify

your voice and provide reinforcement in spaces where you may not always be present.

Advocating for yourself isn't about ego but preserving your presence and influence. By commanding the center with intention, you demonstrate your value while setting the tone for how your contributions are perceived.

Positioning the Queen to Shine

Like the queen's strategic moves, Black women must actively seek high-visibility projects. But choosing the right projects is vital, not all visibility is helpful. The goal is to work on initiatives that allow you to demonstrate your strengths in meaningful ways, aligning with influential stakeholders and company objectives.

In one role, I volunteered for a cross-functional project that matched my strengths and the company's strategic focus. It was challenging but well-aligned, allowing me to show my skills without risking burnout on less impactful tasks. This kind of visibility isn't about being everywhere; it's about being where it counts, reinforcing your value without sacrificing your energy.

Rule Insights

Rule 3: Their best is your mediocre. For Black women, exceeding expectations often becomes the baseline. Strategically choosing high-impact projects ensures your efforts are recognized as exceptional rather than taken for granted.

Rule 5: Goalpost's gonna keep shifting. Selective visibility allows you to adapt to changing organizational priorities, positioning yourself in roles that matter most while sidestepping tasks that add little to your growth or reputation.

Strategy for Success

To position yourself where your value is unmistakable, follow these steps:

- ✓ Select impactful projects: Seek initiatives that align with your strengths and the company's strategic goals, maximizing your contributions and ensuring your efforts are noticed by key stake-holders.

✓ Evaluate the opportunity: Consider whether a project enhances your skills, builds valuable connections, or aligns with your career aspirations before committing.

✓ Avoid overextending: Say no to tasks that dilute your energy or don't advance your long-term objectives, focusing instead on fewer, high-quality opportunities.

✓ Highlight your role: Ensure your contributions are visible by sharing progress and results in meetings or follow-ups, tying your efforts to the initiative's success.

✓ Build relationships strategically: Use high-visibility projects as opportunities to network with decision-makers, positioning yourself for future opportunities.

Strategic positioning is about choosing when and where to show up. By aligning your efforts with projects that truly matter, you create a reputation of purposeful impact while safeguarding your energy and focus.

Surrounding the Queen With Allies

A queen's strength on the chessboard doesn't lie solely in her power — it's amplified by the pieces supporting her. The same principle applies in corporate spaces: building a network of allies strengthens your ability to navigate challenges, expand your influence, and seize opportunities. For Black women, this often means being intentional about identifying those who recognize your value and are willing to advocate for you, particularly in spaces where you're not present. Allies don't just bolster your position — they help ensure your voice and contributions are acknowledged in environments where they might otherwise be overlooked.

I vividly recall a moment early in my career when the importance of alliances became clear. I was part of a high-visibility project and delivered results exceeding expectations. However, my contributions were minimized during a

222

leadership meeting I wasn't invited to. A senior colleague who had seen my work firsthand spoke up on my behalf, ensuring my efforts received the recognition they deserved. Her advocacy shifted the narrative and opened doors to future opportunities. It taught me a critical lesson: having the right allies isn't just helpful, it's essential for navigating spaces where your work and worth may be underappreciated.

Rule Insights

Rule 1: Nobody talks about playing the game. The unspoken dynamics of corporate spaces often revolve around influence and relationships. Having allies ensures you're not navigating the board alone, especially when decisions are made behind closed doors.

Rule 6: Shade is inevitable. Allies provide a buffer against negativity and bias, offering support and validation in spaces where microaggressions or resistance might otherwise overshadow your efforts.

Nicole S. Palmer

Strategy for Success

Building a solid network of allies doesn't happen overnight. It requires intentionality and authenticity:

- ✓ Seek diverse allies: Build relationships across departments, levels, and backgrounds. A varied network ensures broader perspectives and support from multiple angles.
- ✓ Leverage mutual respect: Approach potential allies by recognizing their expertise and contributions, fostering relationships based on mutual value and collaboration.
- ✓ Make your value visible: Share your achievements and goals with allies, equipping them with the information they need to advocate for you effectively.
- ✓ Show reciprocity: Advocacy is a two-way street. Support your allies' initiatives and goals when opportunities arise, reinforcing the partnership.
- ✓ Nurture key relationships: Regularly check in with your allies,

keeping the connection authentic and aligned with shared values and objectives.

Allies are more than colleagues — they're strategic partners who amplify your presence, protect your reputation, and advocate for your success. By surrounding yourself with individuals who see and support your worth, you're building a network that reinforces your position and strengthens your path forward.

Extending Your Reach Across the Board

The queen's power in chess lies in her ability to move across the board with confidence and versatility, impacting multiple areas at once. This translates to showcasing your expertise and establishing yourself as a thought leader in the workplace. This act is especially critical for Black women, as our expertise is often scrutinized or questioned. Proactively demonstrating your knowledge and skills counters biases and ensures your contributions are visible and undeniable.

In one role, I noticed hesitation from colleagues when they sought input or feedback on projects. It became clear that underlying doubts about my capabilities were holding them back. Rather than letting those doubts linger, I took the initiative to lead a training session on a process improvement I had developed. I turned skepticism into respect by explaining the process and answering questions in real time. The training didn't just prove my expertise, it reframed how I was seen in the organization, making me the go-to person for future challenges.

Rule Insights

Rule 3: Their best is your mediocre. Showcasing expertise is one way to ensure your excellence isn't overlooked or undervalued.

Rule 7: Ain't nobody coming to save you. Waiting for others to acknowledge your skills can leave you wanting. Proactively demonstrating your knowledge ensures your expertise is seen, valued, and respected.

Strategy for Success

Extending your reach isn't about showing off, it's about sharing value and creating impact. Use these strategies to establish yourself as a thought leader:

- ✓ Take initiative: Volunteer to lead
  projects, give presentations, or
  share insights during meetings.
  Stepping forward positions you as
  a resource within your organization.
- ✓ Identify key opportunities: Focus
  on areas where your expertise
  aligns with organizational goals
  or where gaps exist. Filling those
  gaps elevates your presence and
  influence.
- ✓ Demonstrate consistency: Expertise isn't proven in a single moment. Consistently show up prepared, insightful, and willing to
  contribute across different settings.
- ✓ Build credibility through education: Offer to lead training ses-
  sions, develop guides, or mentor
  colleagues. Sharing knowledge
  positions you as an authority and

enhances your professional reputation.

✓ Amplify your voice: If possible, contribute to industry conversations through blogs, panels, or social media platforms. Show that your expertise extends beyond your immediate workplace.

Taking up space with your expertise is more than just about proving yourself. It's about owning and using your value to make a meaningful impact. By intentionally extending your reach, you reinforce your reputation as a thought leader while dismantling doubts before they can form.

Communicate Consistently

The queen's power on the chessboard is her versatility and steady influence over the game. Similarly, maintaining consistent communication in the workplace ensures that your contributions remain visible, and your professional narrative stays in your control. This consistency is crucial for Black women in environments where achievements may be minimized or misattributed. Regular communication lets you own your narrative and keep your impact front and center.

Imagine you're leading a cross-departmental project, and midway through, priorities shift. Your team adapts to the changes, but leadership isn't directly involved in the day-to-day operations. Without regular communication, there's a risk that leadership could misinterpret delays as a lack of progress or overlook your team's ability to adapt to evolving needs. By consistently sharing concise updates—highlighting challenges, solutions, and progress—you keep leadership informed, ensuring your efforts are recognized, and misconceptions don't take root.

Rule Insights

Rule 3: Their best is your mediocre. While others may be celebrated for doing the bare minimum, Black women must go the extra mile to highlight their excellence. Regular updates reinforce the value of your contributions.

Rule 7: Ain't nobody coming to save you. Recognition isn't automatic, often your responsibility to ensure your contributions are seen. Consistent communication serves as a safeguard, keeping your achievements in plain sight.

Strategy for Success

Effective communication is more than just providing updates — it involves strategically positioning your contributions to align with organizational goals and priorities.

- ✓ Set a rhythm: Establish a regular cadence for updates, whether weekly, biweekly, or monthly, ensuring leadership and stakeholders stay informed about your progress.
- ✓ Be concise but impactful: Focus on key achievements, tying your updates to measurable outcomes or broader organizational goals. Avoid overwhelming with unnecessary detail.
- ✓ Leverage multiple channels: Share updates via emails, meetings, or team briefings. Diversifying your communication ensures

that your message reaches all necessary audiences.

✓ Highlight your role: Frame updates in a way that emphasizes
your unique contributions without diminishing the team's collective effort.

✓ Seek feedback: Regularly seek input on your updates to ensure
they remain relevant and impactful. Adjust based on your audience's needs.

✓ Document everything: Keep a record of your communications and
milestones. This helps with performance reviews and strengthens your ability to counter
misattributions or challenges to
your work.

Consistent communication is about
building a narrative of value and reliability. By keeping your contributions visible, you ensure that your professional
story is one you control, not written by
others.

Commanding the Center With Intention

Taking center stage isn't about simply being visible, it's about purposeful presence like the queen dominating the chessboard. For Black women, commanding the center means advocating for your worth, leveraging your skills strategically, and aligning your presence with your professional goals. It requires navigating the tightrope of visibility — enough to showcase your impact but not so much that it invites undue scrutiny or bias. This balance isn't just about your career; it's about reshaping the perception of leadership for Black women in corporate spaces.

Imagine being asked to lead a high-profile presentation to senior executives. This opportunity could raise your visibility but also put you under heightened scrutiny. Instead of approaching it cautiously, you prepare meticulously, align your key points with organizational priorities, and tie your insights to measurable outcomes. You balance authority with approachability during the presentation, commanding attention while inviting collaboration. By doing so, you not only deliver results but leave a lasting impression as a confident and capable leader.

Rule Insights

Rule 4: There can only be one. The scarcity mindset often makes it feel like visibility for one Black woman diminishes opportunities for others. Taking center stage with intention combats this narrative, demonstrating that excellence isn't finite.

Rule 7: Ain't nobody coming to save you. Waiting for recognition or opportunities won't serve you. By stepping into the spotlight with purpose, you ensure your contributions and value are undeniable.

Strategy for Success

Commanding the center is about aligning your visibility with strategic goals while maintaining authenticity.

- ✓ Be selective with opportunities: Focus on high-impact roles or projects that align with your strengths and long-term objectives. Avoid spreading yourself thin on tasks that don't advance your career.

✓ Lead with results: Ground your visibility in measurable impact whenever you take center stage. Let your achievements speak for themselves while framing them in ways that align with the organization's goals.

✓ Build a support network: Surround yourself with allies and mentors who amplify your influence. A strong network can provide guidance, advocacy, and reinforcement when the spotlight feels overwhelming.

✓ Stay prepared: Anticipate challenges or biases that may arise and be ready with facts, results, and a straightforward narrative that supports your presence.

✓ Strike the balance: Maintain confidence and authority without alienating colleagues. Commanding the center means being collaborative yet self-assured, striking the right tone for the audience and situation.

✓ Own your narrative: Control how your contributions are perceived by regularly communicating your impact and aligning your work with broader organizational priorities.

Commanding the center with intention isn't just about being seen, it's about shaping how you're seen. By stepping into high-visibility roles with purpose and clarity, you ensure that your presence and contributions leave a lasting, meaningful mark.

Key Takeaways

❖ Advocate Unapologetically: Taking up space is not only your right; it's essential. Assert your achievements confidently, grounding them in the results and impact you bring.

❖ Seek Strategic Visibility: Not all attention is beneficial. Focus on high-impact projects where your contributions align with the organization's goals and amplify your expertise.

❖ Build Your Network of Support: Surround yourself with allies who can support your journey and see your value. True strength in the workplace often comes from a community that amplifies your efforts.

Food for Thought

❖ **Reflect:** What are the areas of your work where your impact isn't fully visible? What small steps can you take to increase recognition in these areas?

❖ **Challenge:** This week, identify a critical project or meeting where your contributions could be more visible. Make a plan to ensure your work is acknowledged through a summary email, presentation, or quick update to leadership.

Chapter 7: Think 10 Steps Ahead

In chess, the best players are always thinking moves ahead, preparing for what's coming before it even appears on the board. They know that every choice influences the next, creating a ripple effect. In corporate America, strategic foresight is your key to staying grounded, resilient, and adaptable, no matter what obstacles or biases you may face. This isn't about living in a state of over-preparation; it's about building a vision that anchors you, giving you the strength to navigate an unpredictable environment with clarity and purpose.

In this chapter, we'll examine cultivating foresight through setting meaningful goals, analyzing trends, managing risks, and building relationships. This isn't just about preparing for challenges — it's about positioning yourself to seize opportunities. It's about staying two steps ahead and holding steady, no matter what moves come your way.

Setting Long-Term Goals

In chess, a queen moves with precision and intent, always working toward a strategy that will secure victory. In your career, setting long-term goals provides that same sense of purpose, keeping you aligned with your aspirations even when external pressures or biases attempt to derail you. Clear objectives act as both a motivator and a compass, reminding you of the bigger picture when day-to-day challenges threaten to pull you off course.

Imagine you're in an entry-level role at a large organization, and your long-term goal is to lead a cross-departmental initiative within five years. Knowing this, you focus on opportunities to build the skills and relationships to attain that goal. You volunteer for projects that expose you to other departments, network strategically, and take on leadership tasks whenever possible. Each decision is deliberate, bringing you closer to that overarching goal, even as circumstances or priorities shift around you. Keeping your long-term objectives in mind ensures that every move is part of a larger strategy.

Rule Insights

Rule 5: Goalpost's gonna keep shifting. In corporate America, the standards and expectations can change on a whim. Long-term goals remain constant in an ever-shifting landscape, ensuring your focus and trajectory remain steady.

Rule 7: Ain't nobody coming to save you. Waiting for others to define your career path won't get you where you want to be. Setting clear goals ensures you're always working toward your vision of success, even when no one else is advocating for you.

Strategy for Success

Defining and pursuing long-term goals allows you to navigate your career purposefully and resiliently.

- ✓ Write down your vision: Articulate what success looks like for you in 5, 10, or even 20 years. Be specific about the roles, skills, or achievements you aim to pursue.

Nicole S. Palmer

✓ Break goals into milestones: Create smaller, achievable steps that keep you moving toward your larger objective, such as completing a certification, expanding your network, or mastering an essential skill.

✓ Stay flexible: Be willing to adjust your goals as circumstances change but never lose sight of your ultimate aspirations. Flexibility ensures you adapt while staying aligned with your vision.

✓ Use setbacks as learning opportunities: View challenges or shifts in your career as chances to refine your approach. Every experience, even a detour, can bring you closer to your long-term goal if framed correctly.

✓ Align daily actions with your goals: Ensure that even your smallest tasks serve your broader vision, whether honing a skill, building relationships, or contributing to high-impact projects.

✓ Revisit and refine: Regularly assess your progress and adjust

240

your goals. Long-term planning is a dynamic process, not a static one.

By setting long-term goals, you take ownership of your career, ensuring every move is deliberate and impactful. Like a queen on the chessboard, your clarity of purpose gives you an advantage, enabling you to navigate with precision and intent.

Seeing Beyond the Next Move

In chess, success often hinges on anticipating your opponent's strategy, not just responding to their immediate move. Similarly, in corporate spaces, recognizing patterns and predicting changes—whether in your organization or industry—positions you as proactive rather than reactive. This foresight is especially critical for Black women in environments where being prepared isn't just an advantage; it's often necessary. Staying ahead means consistently watching for shifts so you're ready to adapt before others even realize a pivot is needed.

Imagine working in an industry where automation and AI are beginning to transform how processes are handled. You notice your organization introducing automation in smaller tasks, signaling a more significant move toward operational efficiency. Instead of waiting to be told to adjust, you proactively take an online course on AI tools and attend webinars on automation's impact in your field. When leadership starts forming a task force to oversee automation integration, you're already positioned as the most knowledgeable team member. This foresight solidifies your relevance and highlights your initiative, earning you a seat at the table before others even realize the table exists.

Rule Insights

Rule 3: Their best is your mediocre. To remain competitive in environments where exceptionalism is the standard for you, you must actively stay ahead of the curve. Anticipating trends ensures you're not just meeting the baseline but consistently exceeding it.

Rule 5: Goalpost's gonna keep shifting. Organizational and industry priorities are constantly evolving. By staying informed, you maintain control over your trajectory, adapting to shifting expectations rather than being caught off guard.

Strategy for Success

Position yourself as a forward-thinking professional by recognizing trends and staying prepared for shifts in priorities.

- ✓ Monitor industry trends: Dedicate time each week to review industry reports, read relevant articles, and follow thought leaders in your field.
- ✓ Track internal shifts: Pay attention to organizational changes, such as new leadership, strategic announcements, or investments in emerging technologies.
- ✓ Build future-proof skills: Identify skills or certifications that align with upcoming trends, ensuring you remain a valuable asset to your team.
- ✓ Stay connected: Join professional groups, attend conferences, and

participate in webinars to remain engaged with the broader conversation in your industry.

✓ Anticipate needs: Look for areas where your team or department may soon need expertise and begin preparing yourself to fill that gap.

✓ Adapt your role: Regularly evaluate how your responsibilities align with evolving priorities and make adjustments to keep yourself at the forefront of organizational goals.

By seeing beyond the next move, you stay relevant and position yourself as a leader who can navigate change with confidence and foresight. Like a chess player anticipating their opponent's strategy, you ensure that every move you make strengthens your position on the board.

Practicing Risk Management

The queen's power in chess is unmatched, but her strength is only as secure as her defenses. In the corporate world, Black women often face heightened risks—whether it's due to company restructuring, shifting priorities, or unforeseen changes in leadership. Practicing risk management isn't about being paranoid; it's about staying vigilant and ready for any outcome. By anticipating potential challenges and planning, you can confidently move through uncertainty, ensuring your career remains resilient no matter what comes your way.

In one role, I caught wind of a possible restructuring in my department. Knowing my role could be impacted, I started networking with leaders in other teams, updated my resume, and took on projects that diversified my skill set. Thanks to my proactive planning, I was prepared to transition smoothly when the restructuring eventually happened. Risk management wasn't about expecting the worst but ensuring I'd be ready to handle it if it came.

Rule Insights

Rule 6: Shade is inevitable. Risk management helps you anticipate potential challenges, including when colleagues or circumstances may work against you. By staying prepared, you ensure that shade always catches you *on* guard.

Rule 1: Nobody talks about playing the game. Understanding the unspoken dynamics of corporate spaces allows you to recognize risks others might not even mention, empowering you to plan your moves before challenges arise.

Strategy for Success

Managing risk isn't about expecting the worst but ensuring you're ready to respond confidently to any challenges.

- ✓ Assess your environment regularly: Identify potential organizational risks, such as leadership turnover, budget changes, or team restructures.
- ✓ Strengthen your network: Cultivate relationships across departments and with leadership, creating a safety net of support.
- ✓ Diversify your skills: Take on projects or training that expand your expertise, ensuring you remain valuable in various roles.

✓ Stay informed: Follow industry trends and company news to anticipate shifts that could impact your position.

✓ Document your achievements: Maintain a clear record of your contributions and accomplishments to bolster your position if changes arise.

✓ Have a plan: Prepare for multiple scenarios, from internal transitions to external opportunities, so you're ready to pivot if needed.

By practicing risk management, you ensure your career remains adaptable and resilient. Like a chess player who plans multiple moves, you can navigate change with intention, knowing that every move you make strengthens your position on the board.

Cultivating Relationships

The support of her surrounding pieces amplifies a queen's strength on the board. In corporate America, relationships play the same role. Connections with allies, mentors, and advocates offer insights, support, and protection. These relationships broaden your perspective and fortify your position, giving you the advocacy you need, especially when challenges arise.

When I set my sights on a strategic role, I knew I needed access to people in decision-making circles. Without direct access to the hiring manager, I built a connection with a colleague who worked closely with that team. We collaborated on a few projects, sharing insights and offering each other support. When a position opened up, she advocated for me, leading to an introduction that eventually paved the way for my transition. Relationships aren't just about being seen, they're about having people who see your potential, even when you're not in the room.

Rule Insights

Rule 6: Shade is inevitable. In a corporate landscape where shade and bias are often unspoken barriers, allies become buffers. Like the queen surrounded by key players, building a network amplifies your reach, helping you stay ahead no matter what challenges come.

Rule 7: Ain't nobody coming to save you. Building a network ensures that when challenges arise, you have people advocating for you in the rooms where decisions are made. Like the queen supported by other pieces, allies extend your influence beyond your immediate reach.

Strategy for Success

Build genuine connections across departments and levels. Allies aren't about self-promotion but creating a network that strengthens your presence and resilience.

- ✓ Seek cross-departmental collaborations that allow you to connect with new colleagues naturally.
- ✓ Identify individuals whose values align with yours and nurture those relationships by offering support and sharing insights.
- ✓ Invest in mentorship as a mentor and mentee to broaden your perspective and create reciprocal value.
- ✓ Look for opportunities to champion others; advocacy is often returned in kind.

✓ Focus on quality over quantity. A few well-placed allies can have a greater impact than a broad network of loose acquaintances.

Relationships are a two-way street; offering support builds trust and reciprocity, which becomes invaluable as you navigate challenges.

Navigating the Board With Foresight

Thinking ten steps ahead isn't about trying to control the future, it's about staying flexible and prepared, no matter what comes next. By setting goals, analyzing patterns, managing risks, and building relationships, you ensure you're never just reacting to what's happening around you; instead, you're moving forward with clear intentions. This foresight is particularly vital for Black women in a landscape where opportunities and challenges can shift unpredictably. This isn't a passive game; it's a strategy for thriving on your terms.

Rule Insights

Rule 1: Nobody talks about playing the game. Foresight is about understanding the unspoken dynamics that shape opportunities. Observing these patterns and preparing accordingly means you're not just surviving—you're actively positioning yourself for success.

Rule 5: Goalpost's gonna keep shifting. In corporate spaces, expectations change frequently, often without notice. Anticipating these shifts lets you stay ahead, always moving toward your long-term objectives, even when the rules change mid-game.

Strategy for Success

Regularly assess your progress, adapt as needed, and stay focused on the bigger picture. Thinking ahead means you're not just here to play the game, you're here to win.

- ✓ Set long-term goals that anchor your decisions and help guide your actions even when challenges arise.

✓ Build a habit of reviewing industry trends, organizational changes, and leadership dynamics to anticipate shifts that may impact your role or goals.

✓ Evaluate your position regularly to ensure you're aligned with opportunities for growth and visibility.

✓ Keep your network strong and diverse so you're well-supported when new challenges or opportunities emerge.

✓ Stay adaptable. If the board changes, be ready to pivot your strategy, ensuring you maintain momentum toward your ultimate objectives.

By thinking ten steps ahead, you create a proactive, intentional path forward — one that ensures every move brings you closer to the career and future you envision.

Key Takeaways

❖ Set intentional goals: Define long-term objectives that align with your values and career vision.

These goals serve as a guiding path, helping you make choices that bring you closer to the future you envision.

❖ Stay ahead of trends: Observing shifts within your industry and organization keeps you adaptable, preparing you to pivot when needed and positioning you as a proactive leader.

❖ Practice resilience through risk management: Anticipating potential challenges and planning accordingly strengthens your ability to handle setbacks without feeling destabilized.

❖ Set long-term goals: Define a clear vision for your career that guides each decision. Periodically reassess these goals to ensure they align with your evolving aspirations.

❖ Analyze trends and patterns: Keep a pulse on industry and organizational shifts, preparing to pivot when needed.

❖ Regularly evaluate potential risks and plan for various outcomes so you're never caught off guard.

❖ Cultivate relationships with key players: Build a network of genuine connections, creating a support system that offers insights, advocacy, and resilience.

Food for Thought

❖ **Reflect:** How do your current role and daily tasks align with your long-term goals? Are there minor adjustments you could make to connect the two better?

❖ **Challenge:** This week, research trends or emerging priorities within your field. Identify one skill or area of knowledge that could increase your value and consider ways to develop it.

Chapter 8: Know Your Opponents

In chess, not every piece is positioned to help you reach your goal; some are there solely to obstruct and challenge you. In the corporate world, it's no different. Certain colleagues and leaders, whether intentional in their actions or not, will become obstacles in your journey. They may not wear their intentions openly, but their influence can hinder progress, creating barriers that often feel as strategic and calculated as moves on a chessboard.

Understanding your opponents is as crucial as understanding your allies. Just as a skilled chess player studies each piece on the board, analyzing potential threats and anticipating moves, navigating the board requires that same level of insight and strategy. Recognizing the adversaries around you helps you understand who may stand in your way so you can respond with measure and foresight. Each archetype represents a unique challenge, shaped by overt actions and discreet maneuvers.

In this chapter, we'll delve into the archetypes of workplace adversaries. These aren't always overt antagonists; sometimes, they present as colleagues, leaders, or even versions of ourselves that quietly undermine our advancement. Each archetype mirrors a piece on the chessboard, ranked by its potential impact on your career trajectory. I've ordered these archetypes based on the negative impact they can inflict, beginning with the most damaging. By understanding their tactics, strengths, and limitations, you'll gain the tools to protect your position, secure your value, and keep moving forward—no matter the challenges ahead.

The Slick Saboteur: The Stealthy Bishop

In chess, bishops move diagonally, often striking from unexpected angles and crossing long stretches of the board with precision. In the workplace, slick saboteurs operate in a similarly indirect way, quietly undermining others without leaving obvious traces. For Black women, the presence of a slick saboteur can be particularly challenging, as their actions often reinforce the idea that Black women are "unfit," "unqualified," or "too aggressive" to succeed. The sabotage isn't overt, which makes it difficult to call out without seeming overly sensitive or paranoid, leaving Black women feeling isolated and disempowered.

Who They Are

Slick saboteurs often present as neutral or supportive colleagues, but their actions consistently create obstacles. These individuals may hold roles in management, team leadership, or even peer-level positions where they have access to key decision-makers and organizational influence. They thrive in environments where their indirect tactics go unnoticed or are excused as "miscommunications" or "oversights."

Their sabotage typically involves behaviors that are difficult to prove or confront directly, creating a gaslighting effect that leaves their targets questioning whether the issue lies with them rather than the saboteur. This ambiguity makes them particularly insidious opponents.

How they Operate

A slick saboteur might use tactics such as withholding important information, undermining others by spreading rumors and half-truths, excluding you from critical conversations, or "forgetting" to loop you into crucial emails. These actions may appear minor in isolation but accumulate over time, creating a perception of incompetence, unpreparedness, or personality flaws. For Black women, who already face heightened scrutiny in the workplace, this kind of sabotage reinforces a perception of underperformance, making it harder to build credibility and demonstrate expertise.

Slick saboteurs often know how to exploit the gaps in organizational structures, taking advantage of biases that may already exist. For example, they might play into stereotypes by framing their indirect actions as "concerns" for the Black woman's professional growth, which, in reality, only serve to limit her access to opportunities. These underhanded tactics create a situation where, even when Black women excel, their achievements can be minimized or questioned due to the environment of doubt that the saboteur has cultivated.

Role on the Board

On the corporate chessboard, the slick saboteur functions as a stealthy bishop, operating from the periphery to influence perceptions and narratives. While they may not have overt power, their indirect actions create ripple effects that impact team dynamics, leadership trust, and individual reputations.

Their role is to maintain the status quo by ensuring that certain individuals, particularly Black women, are seen as less competent or less deserving of advancement. This makes them formidable opponents who can shape organizational narratives in subtle yet damaging ways.

I once had a colleague who consistently failed to share important project updates, often leading to last-minute changes that left me scrambling to catch up. The pattern was subtle but deliberate, creating an impression that I was always one step behind. I adjusted my approach when I began to see this as a form of sabotage. I started confirming project details directly with our manager and proactively shared updates with the team, creating a record of my preparedness. Over time, this proactive transparency made it clear where the issue truly lay, protecting my reputation and showing that I was on top of my responsibilities.

Rule Insights

Rule 2: There are no spectators. In a corporate environment, where we are often judged more harshly, the presence of a slick saboteur reminds us that nothing goes unnoticed. Even when intentions aren't clear, every move on the board has an impact, and it's essential to remain vigilant, ensuring that one's efforts and integrity are consistently visible.

Strategy for Success

To navigate and neutralize a slick saboteur, consider these actionable steps:

- ✓ Document everything: Keep a detailed record of interactions, project updates, and decisions to create a clear trail of your contributions and communication.

✓ Proactively share updates: Regularly communicate your progress with team leads and stakeholders to ensure your work is visible and can't be undermined.

✓ Confirm and clarify: Follow up on verbal agreements or missing communications with written confirmations: "Just following up to confirm we're aligned on…"

✓ Leverage allies: Build transparency with trusted colleagues and mentors who can advocate on your behalf and corroborate your contributions.

✓ Call out exclusion diplomatically: If excluded from meetings or updates, address it professionally: "I noticed I wasn't included. Can you confirm if there are updates I should be aware of?"

✓ Reinforce credibility: Consistently deliver high-quality work, leaving little room for others to question your capabilities.

✓ Stay composed: Avoid emotional confrontations; address issues calmly and with evidence, maintaining professionalism at all times.

The Cunning Confidant: The Dubious Pawn

Pawns may seem harmless in chess, but under the right conditions, they can shift the board and impact the game significantly. The cunning confidant operates similarly in the workplace. Positioned in entry- or mid-level roles, they often present themselves as allies, confidants, or colleagues who understand your perspective. However, they have an agenda, using the information you share to advance their goals — sometimes at your expense.

Who They Are

Cunning confidants often exist in roles where they're close enough to see the challenges you face but not necessarily positioned to provide direct support. They might be a peer, a teammate, or even a mentor figure who seems sympathetic. Their outward friendliness and willingness to listen can make you feel safe confiding in them. However, unlike a genuine ally, the cunning confidant's motivations are self-serving. They may use your shared experiences as fuel to elevate their standing, leverage your insights for personal gain, or align themselves with higher-ups by positioning you as a rival.

For Black women, the cunning confidant is particularly insidious when they are a fellow Black woman. This shared identity can create a sense of solidarity and mutual understanding, leading you to let down your guard, believing that you're both navigating the same challenges. However, the reality can be far more complex and, ultimately, painful. This confidant might be driven by a scarcity mentality, feeling that there's only room for one Black woman at the top, and therefore sees you as competition rather than as a sister in the same struggle. Recognizing this type of cunning confidant requires discernment and a willingness to protect yourself, even when it feels counterintuitive.

How They Operate

Like pawns on a chessboard, the cunning confidant moves in seemingly small but calculated ways. They may start by positioning themselves as a trusted colleague, sharing their own experiences to create a bond. Over time, they encourage you to open up, slyly gathering details about your struggles, ambitions, or frustrations. Once they've amassed enough information, they deploy it strategically — often in ways that aren't immediately obvious.

When the cunning confidant is a fellow Black woman, the betrayal cuts deeper because it undermines the sense of sisterhood that is often a source of strength in challenging environments. This confidant may present herself as someone who "gets it," making you believe you're in it together. However, she may then turn around and use your experiences as leverage to gain favor with those in power, positioning herself as the "good fit" while framing you as less competent, less agreeable, or even as a "difficult." This dual loyalty enables her to play both sides, appearing supportive while quietly advancing her agenda—or even aligning herself with others who may not have your best interests at heart.

A cunning confidant might:

- Mirror your vulnerabilities to build trust: They may share fabricated or exaggerated struggles of their own, creating a false sense of solidarity.
- Reframe private conversations: Your shared ideas or insights may resurface in meetings or discussions, slightly altered, as if they were hers.
- Sow subtle doubt about your character: Comments like "I'm sure she meant well, but…" can plant seeds of doubt among colleagues or leadership.
- Leverage relationships for personal gain: They may align with influential figures, framing their connection with you as mentorship rather than collaboration.
- Redirect opportunities: Under the guise of support, they may "recommend" opportunities that steer

you away from your goals while placing themselves in prime positions.

- Weaponize shared struggles: They might downplay systemic challenges you've discussed in private while positioning themselves as someone who can easily navigate those challenges, elevating their reputation at your expense.

Imagine working in a competitive department, and a new Black colleague joins your team. You're excited, feeling a natural camaraderie and relief to have someone who shares your background and understands the complexities you face. Over time, you begin to confide in her about your challenges, frustrations, and aspirations. She listens, nods empathetically, and shares similar stories of her own.

However, as time passes, you start noticing some changes. She mentions things in meetings that mirror ideas you shared privately but reframes them to make herself look insightful. Worse, she begins forming alliances with senior leaders, positioning herself as more "aligned" with the company culture. Meanwhile, she heavily implies that you're overly ambitious or outspoken, sowing doubts about your suitability for future leadership roles. You realize that the bond you thought was genuine was, in fact, a tool she used to gather insights she could weaponize to elevate herself.

Role on the Board

On the corporate chessboard, the cunning confidant functions as a dubious pawn, leveraging their perceived innocence to maneuver in ways that catch others off guard. While they may lack formal power, they use relationships and trust as their primary tools to influence the board. Their role is particularly harmful because it's built on betrayal—using trust as a weapon to undermine their targets while advancing their position.

For us, the cunning confidant is especially damaging because their actions can erode trust not only with the confidant but also within broader professional relationships. The fallout of their tactics often leaves the target isolated and questioning whether anyone in the organization can be trusted.

In these cases, it can be one of the most challenging and disheartening opponents to navigate. They operate under the guise of empathy, but their intentions are self-serving.

Rule Insights

Rule 4: There can only be one. This archetype plays directly into the scarcity mentality embedded in many corporate spaces, where it often feels like there's only room for one Black woman in a position of influence or visibility. The cunning confidant, especially when she is a fellow Black woman, may exploit this dynamic, viewing you as competition rather than a potential ally. Instead of seeing mutual success as achievable, she benefits from the unspoken "one-at-a-time" rule, reinforcing barriers rather than breaking them. Recognizing this mentality helps you approach cautiously, understanding that not all shared experiences equate to shared loyalties.

Strategy for Success

To navigate and counteract the cunning confidant, use this checklist to protect yourself:

✓ Assess trust carefully: Avoid assuming shared identity equals shared intentions. Take time to observe their actions before confiding in them.

✓ Guard your information: Be selective about what you share, especially your ambitions, challenges, or personal strategies.

✓ Test their intentions: First, share non-essential, low-stakes information and monitor how they handle it before trusting them with sensitive details.

✓ Keep documentation: Maintain a record of your key conversations, decisions, and accomplishments. This ensures that your work is attributed to you.

✓ Strengthen other relationships: Build a network of trusted allies who can offer genuine support and balance the potential harm of the confidant's actions.

✓ Stay professional: If their betrayal becomes apparent, avoid emotional reactions. Instead, address issues calmly and through formal channels, if necessary.

✓ Focus on your goals: Redirect your energy toward your growth and success, ensuring the confidant's actions don't derail your progress.

The Blockade Boss: The Restrictive King

In chess, the king is the centerpiece of the game, the most protected and guarded piece on the board, representing ultimate authority and control. In the workplace, the blockade boss plays a similar role. They are the decision-makers, the policy-setters, and the ultimate arbiters of access and opportunity. However, for Black women, the blockade boss often becomes a symbol of systemic challenges. They can dictate the trajectory of careers by grant-ing—or denying—critical opportunities.

This archetype is not always inherently malicious but operates as a function of the broader system. Their decisions, biases (conscious or unconscious), and influence often reinforce the status quo, creating an environment where access to leadership, visibility, and high-impact projects feels out of reach. Navigating the blockade boss requires a blend of strategic relationship-building, adaptability, and persistence.

Who They Are

The blockade boss is usually in a position of significant authority within the organization: executives, directors, or senior managers. Their power lies in their ability to grant access to opportunities like promotions, key assignments, or organizational resources.

While some blockade bosses may actively champion inclusion, others operate from a scarcity mindset or implicit biases that prevent them from seeing the full value of diverse talent. For Black women, this often means jumping through additional hoops to prove competency, navigating coded language about "fit," or encountering decisions rooted in optics rather than merit.

How They Operate

Blockade bosses exert their power in visible and subtle ways, often shaping the environment for everyone around them. Their influence can be wielded as a tool for support or as a barrier to progress.

Common tactics include:

- Selective Gatekeeping: Providing opportunities to a select few while blocking access for others based on perceived fit, bias, or favoritism.
- Tokenism: Elevating a single individual to maintain the illusion of inclusivity while withholding broader systemic change.
- Shifting Expectations: Changing the benchmarks for success or redefining roles to maintain control over who advances.

- Undermining Credibility: Questioning or downplaying achievements subtly to limit visibility and growth.
- Maintaining the Status Quo: Choosing inaction over active support for equity, reinforcing existing power structures.

For example, imagine a senior manager who controls access to a high-stakes project. While claiming to value diverse perspectives, they consistently overlook your contributions, assigning key responsibilities to others. They might frame this as giving you time to "grow" or "gain experience," all while denying you the very opportunities that would allow you to demonstrate your capabilities.

When the Blockade Boss Is Your Supervisor

The challenges escalate when the Blockade Boss is not just a figure of influence but your direct supervisor. They hold the reins of your day-to-day trajectory, and their decisions often shape how leadership views your readiness, potential, and future. This power dynamic requires careful navigation to avoid being defined by their limitations. While their authority may seem all-encompassing, there are deliberate steps you can take to navigate their influence and advocate for your growth without jeopardizing your professional standing.

Engage in skip-level conversations. If your supervisor consistently blocks your access to growth opportunities, consider engaging with their manager tactfully. This requires framing the conversation around your professional development rather than criticizing your supervisor:

- "I'd love your insight on how I can continue to grow and align my work with the broader goals of the organization."

By focusing on your goals and organizational impact, you can create visibility for your contributions without making the conversation confrontational.

Build visibility beyond your boss. When the blockade boss restricts your access, look for ways to contribute to cross-functional projects or organizational initiatives that expose your work to others. Building relationships outside your team ensures that your value is seen and appreciated beyond the lens of one individual.

Document and communicate wins. Create a consistent record of your accomplishments and contributions. Share regular updates that align your work with the company's broader goals. A well-placed email or team update can demonstrate your impact and provide clarity for others who might otherwise rely solely on your supervisor's perspective.

Know when to pivot. There are times when persistence is not enough. If your supervisor consistently undermines your progress, exploring other opportunities within or outside the organization may be necessary. Transitioning isn't a failure — it's a strategic decision to prioritize your growth.

Role on the Board

On the corporate chessboard, the Blockade Boss represents ultimate control over the game's trajectory. While the King's moves are limited in chess, their power lies in their ability to command the board through the support of other pieces. Similarly, the Blockade Boss in corporate spaces uses their influence to determine who has access to critical opportunities and advancement.

For Black women, the blockade boss's decisions often create significant hurdles. Whether intentional or unconscious, their actions — or inaction — can reinforce systemic inequities, shaping the narrative of who "deserves" to lead, contribute, or be seen.

Rule Insights

Rule 1: Nobody talks about playing the game. The blockade boss exemplifies the unspoken nature of the rules. Their decisions are rarely transparent, and their expectations are often unclear. Recognizing this reality allows you to approach them strategically, building relationships and leveraging allies to navigate their influence effectively.

Rule 5: Goalpost's gonna keep shifting. Blockade bosses often move the target, redefining what success looks like or adding new hurdles just when you think you've met the mark. Understanding this dynamic helps you stay prepared and flexible, ensuring you're always ready to advocate for yourself.

Strategy for Success

Navigating the blockade boss requires a mix of self-advocacy, strategic alliances, and adaptability. Use these actionable steps to position yourself effectively:

- ✓ Document Your Achievements: Keep a detailed record of your contributions, aligning them with organizational goals to demonstrate your value clearly.
- ✓ Build Strategic Relationships: Develop connections with colleagues, mentors, and allies who can advocate for you and provide access to opportunities outside the Blockade Boss's control.
- ✓ Communicate Proactively: Share your progress and achievements directly with leadership, ensuring your work is visible and recognized.
- ✓ Ask for Clarity: When expectations or opportunities are unclear, seek direct feedback: "What would success in this role look like, and how can I align my efforts to achieve it?"

✓ Leverage Allies: Partner with mentors or sponsors who can provide insight into the Blockade Boss's perspective and help amplify your voice.

✓ Stay Persistent: Don't let setbacks define your journey. Use every interaction as an opportunity to refine your approach and demonstrate resilience.

✓ Know When to Pivot: If the Blockade Boss consistently blocks your progress, explore other paths within or outside the organization to achieve your goals.

The blockade boss is a formidable opponent, but their power is not absolute. By staying strategic, focused, and aligned with your long-term goals, you can navigate their influence and ensure your value is seen, even in the most challenging environments. Recognize their role on the board and position yourself to win, knowing that your journey doesn't end

279

with their approval—it continues with your determination.

The Relentless Rival: The Opposing Rook

In chess, the rook moves in straight, powerful lines, aiming to dominate and control space. Relentless rivals in the workplace operate similarly: they're clear in their ambition and may openly vie for the same clients, projects, or promotions. Their strategy often involves overshadowing your work or attempting to claim shared successes as their own. For Black women, the relentless rival goes beyond a mere individual to represent the structural reality that often limits how many Black women can occupy influential roles. This scarcity, rooted in the unspoken "There can only be one" rule, can create an environment where competition feels heightened, as both you and your competitor know that opportunities for advancement are limited.

In many cases, relentless rivals may perceive your presence as a direct threat, especially if they view you as someone who doesn't "fit the mold" of who should be in the room. This archetype often leverages their proximity to power, seniority, or privilege to position themselves as the more "acceptable" choice for leadership roles. They may use their visibility to downplay your contributions or position your ideas as secondary to their own.

For Black women, dealing with a relentless rival can mean advocating for your work and countering the biases that place your achievements under a harsher lens. While others may be celebrated for their ambition and assertiveness, Black women are often seen as "too aggressive" or "difficult," a double standard that relentless rivals can exploit. In many ways, these competitors serve as gatekeepers, controlling the narrative and shaping others' perceptions of you based on limited access to leadership.

Who They Are

Relentless rivals are often peers or slightly senior colleagues who are ambitious and focused on advancement. They tend to view their success as a zero-sum game, meaning your progress is perceived as a direct threat to theirs. They often occupy roles with high visibility, giving them the proximity and access to position themselves favorably with leadership.

While relentless rivals may see themselves as simply "competitive," their actions often cross the line into undermining others. They may use their visibility to claim credit for shared successes, frame your ideas as less impactful than their own, or amplify perceptions of you as a "poor fit" for leadership. This archetype is particularly damaging because they often operate openly, disguising their undermining behavior as "healthy competition."

For Black women, the relentless rival dynamic is further exacerbated by systemic biases that reinforce the idea that only one Black woman can succeed in a given space. This creates a heightened sense of competition, where the stakes feel disproportionately high for both individuals.

How They Operate

Relentless rivals operate like rooks on a chessboard: their moves are direct, calculated, and aimed at controlling space. They rarely work covertly — instead, their strategies are often visible but difficult to confront without appearing defensive or confrontational. This visibility makes them incredibly challenging to navigate.

A relentless rival might:

- Claim shared successes as their own: They often frame team efforts or collaborative ideas as their sole contributions.
- Downplay your contributions: They may subtly imply that your work is less impactful or that your ideas lack merit.
- Leverage proximity to power: By aligning closely with senior leaders or decision-makers, they position themselves as the "logical" choice for opportunities.
- Exploit biases: Relentless rivals may amplify existing stereotypes or biases, framing you as "too aggressive," "unapproachable," or

> "not a team player" to diminish
> your credibility.

The key to understanding their tactics is to recognize that their behavior isn't just about competition, it's about eliminating perceived threats. This means they'll often target high-performing and well-regarded individuals, knowing that these individuals pose the greatest challenge to their advancement.

Role on the Board

On the corporate chessboard, the relentless rival serves as an opposing rook—a piece with the power to dominate and control space through direct, forceful moves. Their primary role is to claim territory, overshadow others, and position themselves as indispensable.

For Black women, the relentless rival can feel like both an opponent and a gatekeeper, as their actions often reinforce structural biases that limit the number of Black women who can occupy positions of influence. Understanding their role is critical to developing strategies that neutralize their impact without sacrificing your integrity or professionalism.

Rule Insights

Rule 2: There are no spectators. In corporate America, every move you make is being watched, whether by rivals, allies, or decision-makers. Relentless rivals often exploit this reality by controlling the narrative and showcasing their value at your expense. Recognizing this dynamic helps you stay vigilant, ensuring your contributions are consistently visible and your reputation remains intact. By actively participating and demonstrating your value, you remove the space for rivals to define your role.

Strategy for Success

To navigate and neutralize a relentless rival, use the following strategies:

- ✓ Document your contributions: Keep detailed records of your work, ensuring your achievements are attributed to you.
- ✓ Communicate proactively: Share your updates and successes directly with leadership, making

your impact visible without waiting for others to acknowledge it.

✓ Cultivate strategic allies: Build relationships with colleagues and mentors who can advocate for you and counterbalance the rival's narrative.

✓ Focus on your unique strengths: Highlight what sets you apart, ensuring your contributions are distinct and not easily overshadowed.

✓ Stay professional under pressure: Avoid reacting emotionally to undermining behavior, which could be used against you. Instead, maintain composure and address issues through appropriate channels.

✓ Leverage feedback: Seek input from trusted mentors or supervisors to ensure your work and contributions are aligned with organizational goals and valued by leadership.

✓ Control the narrative: When possible, preemptively share your ideas and achievements in public forums, such as team meetings, to

establish yourself as a key contrib-
utor.

The Evasive Encroacher: The Elusive Knight

In chess, the knight is known for its
unique L-shaped movement, leaping over
obstacles and reaching places other pieces
can't. The evasive encroacher in the workplace embodies this same elusive, indirect
style of influence. They rarely confront
you directly but instead rely on subtle,
passive-aggressive tactics that undermine
you in unpredictable and often covert
ways. Their moves are hard to anticipate
and even harder to counter without seeming overly sensitive or confrontational—
two perceptions Black women are frequently cautious to avoid.

For Black women, the evasive encroacher
presents a particularly insidious challenge. This archetype might make seemingly innocuous comments that cast
doubt on your ideas, subtly imply that
you're overstepping, or even suggest that
your approach is "too ambitious" or "too

much." These comments are rarely outright, leaving you questioning your perceptions. You might wonder if you're imagining slights or over-interpreting their actions, which can chip away at your confidence over time.

The evasive encroacher's tactics are often so unassuming that they can be easily dismissed as minor, incidental behaviors by others — creating a workplace where their undermining goes unchecked. In meetings, they might casually mention trivial flaws in your work, but when added up, they cast you in a less favorable light. They exclude you from critical emails, conveniently leave you out of meetings, or "helpfully" remind you to double-check things as though your competence is in question. These small actions add up to a pattern of erosion, subtly impacting your credibility and, by extension, your advancement.

This type of undermining can create a precarious balancing act because we are often subjected to higher scrutiny and expectations. Calling out passive-aggressive behavior can carry additional risk, as it may be interpreted as overreacting or overly defensive. Maintaining professionalism while countering an evasive encroacher's veiled attacks is mentally taxing, adding an extra layer of pressure in environments where trust is already hard to secure.

Who They Are

Evasive encroachers are often colleagues in similar or adjacent roles, positioned close enough to observe your work but not directly accountable for your success. They may be peers, junior team members, or even supervisors, often using their familiarity with your role to question your performance subtly.

These individuals thrive in ambiguity. They rarely take clear stances or engage directly in conflicts, relying instead on underhanded tactics to undermine you. Their behavior is rooted in insecurity, a desire for control, or a need to maintain a certain level of perceived superiority in the workplace. For Black women, the challenge lies in navigating the encroacher's indirect actions without

escalating tensions or confirming stereotypes of being "overly sensitive."

How They Operate

Like knights on a chessboard, evasive encroachers rely on moves that are difficult
to predict and counter. Their tactics are
subtle but consistent, designed to erode
confidence and credibility over time without leaving apparent evidence of their intent.

Common strategies include:

- Subtle criticisms: Offering backhanded compliments or nitpick-
  ing small details to doubt your
  competence.
- Exclusionary behavior: Leaving
  you out of crucial meetings, email
  chains, or decisions and framing it
  as an oversight.
- Feigning support: Phrasing undermining comments as "helpful"
  suggestions or concerns about
  your approach.
- Shifting narratives: Using ambiguity to rewrite the context of

events or conversations, often to
their advantage.

These behaviors often leave you questioning your perceptions, wondering whether
the slight was intentional or a misunderstanding. This uncertainty is part of their
strategy, discouraging confrontation and
enabling their behavior to continue unchecked.

Let's say you're part of a team where a
colleague frequently makes offhand comments in meetings, praising parts of your
work but hinting at minor oversights in
private follow-ups. For example, they
might say, "I just thought you'd want to
double-check this detail next time," im-
plying a need for extra vigilance that feels
subtly condescending. Rather than confronting them publicly, respond professionally and acknowledge their "helpful"
suggestions while sharing your progress
with a trusted ally or supervisor. In doing
so, you maintain control over the narrative, reinforcing your reliability and protecting yourself from one-sided criticisms.

Role on the Board

The evasive encroacher acts as an elusive knight on the corporate chessboard, disrupting your path and creating obstacles that aren't immediately visible. Their role is to sow doubt and destabilize your position, often operating just outside the bounds of accountability.

For Black women, the evasive encroacher represents a unique challenge because their indirect tactics align with broader systemic biases. This combination can amplify feelings of isolation and self-doubt, making it harder to navigate workplace dynamics confidently. Recognizing their role is essential to countering their impact effectively.

Rule Insights

Rule 5: Goalpost's Gonna keep shifting. Evasive encroachers are masters at subtly turning the standards or expectations, making you feel as though you're constantly adjusting to their veiled criticisms. This feeling is often all too familiar: the bar is continuously moving, and we're constantly being measured against standards designed to keep us off balance.

Strategy for Success

Navigating the evasive encroacher requires a calm, strategic approach to protect your credibility while minimizing unnecessary conflict. Use the following strategies:

- ✓ Observe and document patterns: Keep track of interactions where their behavior undermines your work. Patterns provide clarity and evidence if escalation becomes necessary.
- ✓ Follow up diplomatically: If excluded from meetings or communications, send a professional follow-up to clarify: "Just checking if there was an update I may have missed."
- ✓ Engage allies: Build relationships with trusted colleagues who can support your work and provide perspective on the encroacher's tactics.
- ✓ Maintain transparency: Share updates and progress with the broader team or supervisors to counter any narrative of incompetence.

- ✓ Reframe criticism: Address "help-ful" suggestions by thanking them and reinforcing your preparation and competency: "Thanks for the input. I've already accounted for that in my approach."
- ✓ Stay professional: Avoid reacting emotionally to their behavior. Re-maining calm and focused protects your reputation while diffusing potential conflict.
- ✓ Prioritize resilience: Recognize that their behavior often reflects their insecurities, not your capabil-ities. Focus on your long-term goals; don't let their tactics derail your progress.

The Silent Symbol: Shadow Queen

The queen is the most powerful chess piece, moving freely across the board with unmatched versatility. But on the board, some high-ranking Black women occupy roles where the title suggests au-thority, yet real power remains out of reach. The shadow queen archetype illus-trates the phenomenon of being positioned as a figurehead: visible in title, symbolic in function. The shadow queen exists in a precarious space where she is seen but not truly heard. She is granted a seat at the table but denied the tools to drive meaningful change.

Becoming the shadow queen is both a triumph and a trap for Black women. The high-ranking title may signify an achievement hard won through resilience and strategic navigation. However, the lack of real influence is a barrier—an unspoken reminder that corporate America values the optics of progress more than the reality of systemic change. Organizations frequently place Black women in these roles to check a box for diversity, using their visibility to signal inclusivity while preserving the status quo.

The emotional toll of this role can be immense. The shadow queen carries the weight of representation, often as the sole Black woman in leadership, yet finds her contributions minimized or dismissed. The dissonance between the expectation to lead and the reality of restricted power creates constant tension, leading to frustration, burnout, and, at times, the difficult decision to leave.

How They Operate

The shadow queen's role is defined by contradiction. She may be invited to meetings with top executives but excluded from key decision-making conversations. Her name may appear on initiatives as a leader, but her recommendations are often watered down or ignored altogether. She is tasked with high-visibility projects — usually related to diversity, equity, and inclusion — yet lacks the authority to influence the broader strategy or allocate resources effectively.

And yet, the shadow queen must navigate these dynamics with precision. She recognizes the limitations of her role but also sees opportunities to wield indirect influence. By aligning with allies who hold actual power, she learns to amplify her voice in subtle but impactful ways. At the same time, she remains hyper-aware of the expectations placed upon her and the scrutiny she faces, balancing the need to fulfill her duties with the necessity of protecting her integrity.

For example, consider a senior executive brought in to lead a significant diversity initiative. Her role seems powerful on paper, with a "Chief" title and broad organizational visibility. Yet, behind the scenes, other executives routinely overridden her ideas, and her access to decision-making forums is nonexistent. Despite her efforts to create meaningful change, she is often reduced to a spokesperson—expected to articulate the company's commitment to progress without the ability to enforce it. Ultimately, she leaves the role, recognizing that her energy and expertise would be better valued elsewhere.

Another common scenario involves Black women promoted to leadership roles during times of crisis—a phenomenon referred to as the "glass cliff." These women are responsible for navigating turbulent waters but are not given the tools, funding, or resources to chart the course out of crisis effectively. Their success is contingent on circumstances outside their control, and when the ship inevitably sinks, they are often scapegoated, reinforcing harmful stereotypes about Black women in leadership.

Rule Insights

Rule 1: Nobody talks about playing the game. The shadow queen's experience underscores the unspoken rules of corporate spaces, where titles and optics often trump real power. Black women in this role are reminded that visibility is not synonymous with influence, and the game is often about maintaining appearances rather than enacting substantive change. Recognizing this rule allows the shadow queen to navigate her position with a clear-eyed understanding of its limitations.

Rule 4: There can only be one. As the lone Black woman in a high-ranking role, the shadow queen often finds herself isolated, held up as a symbol of progress while being denied the tools to make it a reality. This singular status reinforces the scarcity model, where organizations create the illusion of inclusion by elevating one individual while neglecting systemic change. The shadow queen must weigh whether her presence in this role serves her goals or perpetuates the "one-at-a-time" mindset.

Rule 5: Goalpost's gonna keep shifting. The shadow queen frequently encounters shifting expectations. One moment, she is expected to be visible and vocal; the next, she is relegated to the background. This inconsistency is draining, especially when paired with the pressure to perform flawlessly in a role that is fundamentally constrained. Understanding this dynamic can help her set boundaries and evaluate when the role no longer aligns with her aspirations.

Strategy for Success

If you find yourself in the role of the shadow queen, it's essential to approach it with clarity and strategy.

- ✓ Recognize the limits of your role: Acknowledge where your influence begins and ends and use this understanding to craft a strategy that maximizes your impact within those boundaries.
- ✓ Leverage your visibility: Advocate for meaningful change by aligning with allies who have actual decision-making power and can amplify your voice.

- ✓ Cultivate genuine alliances: Build relationships with colleagues who respect and value your contributions, extending your network beyond the confines of your immediate role.
- ✓ Set clear boundaries: Protect your energy by engaging only in projects that align with your principles and avoiding situations where your presence is leveraged for optics rather than substance.
- ✓ Monitor your long-term goals: Regularly evaluate whether the role aligns with your aspirations, and don't hesitate to seek opportunities where your expertise will be fully recognized.
- ✓ Control the narrative: Be intentional about presenting your accomplishments and vision, ensuring your value is apparent even in an environment that may downplay your influence.
- ✓ Know when to exit: Understand that leaving a role that doesn't serve you is not a failure but a

strategic move toward a more fulfilling and impactful career.

Above all, remember that being a shadow queen does not reflect your capabilities but the corporate structures that continue to grapple with genuine inclusivity. Approach this role with patience, perspective, and the understanding that your journey does not end here. Empower yourself by seeking opportunities that align with your vision for meaningful impact, knowing that your value transcends the limitations of any one position.

Key Takeaways

❖ Understand Archetypes: Recognizing workplace archetypes like the cunning confidant, slick saboteur, and evasive encroacher helps you anticipate challenges and respond strategically.

❖ Don't Take It Personally: Remember, your opponents' actions often reflect their insecurities or agendas, not your worth or abilities. Focus on neutralizing their impact, not on proving yourself to them.

- ❖ Leverage Emotional Intelligence: Approach opponents with calm and intentionality. Anticipate their moves and motivations, using observation and strategy to maintain control.
- ❖ Build Strong Allies: A robust support network helps buffer against adversarial actions, ensu-ring you're not navigating these dynamics alone.
- ❖ Play the Long Game: Use every encounter with an opponent as a learning opportunity. Observing patterns and behaviors builds your ability to navigate challenges over time.
- ❖ Document Interactions: Keep records of key conversations and incidents involving your oppo-nents. This will help you maintain clarity and reinforce your narrative when needed.
- ❖ Establish Your Presence: Combat attempts to undermine your influence by making your contributions and value visible to leadership and peers.

Food for Thought

- ❖ **Reflect:** Have you encountered a workplace opponent recently? Identify their archetype and consider how their behavior affected your work approach. Could a shift in strategy improve the dynamic?
- ❖ **Challenge:** This week, document interactions with a colleague whose actions have raised concerns. Reflect on their potential motivations and plan one specific action you can take to neutralize their influence.

Nicole S. Palmer

Chapter 9: Build Your Defense

In chess, a solid defense is crucial for survival. It's what keeps you stable and shields you from unexpected attacks. Building a solid defense in corporate America means more than just safeguarding your position. It's about protecting your mental and emotional well-being, defending your reputation, and ensuring that you have the room to make empowered choices in any situation. A rock-solid defense is essential for survival and thriving for Black women, who often face heightened scrutiny and unique challenges.

This chapter outlines defensive strategies for fortifying your career and maintaining resilience. Think of each strategy as another layer in your armor, designed to keep you steady and prepared for whatever comes your way.

Note on Navigating HR

While some may view HR as part of a defense strategy, the reality for Black women is often more nuanced. Trusting HR—or navigating its limitations—requires strategies beyond this chapter's scope. Here, we focus on tools you can control personally: fortifying your boundaries, building financial and emotional resilience, and preparing for unforeseen challenges. HR-specific strategies will be explored in-depth in *Surviving the Game While Black Womaning in Corporate America*™, where we'll unpack how to navigate HR while protecting your career and well-being.

Fortifying Professional Boundaries

Pawns form chess's first line of defense, creating a protective boundary that guards more powerful pieces. In corporate life, boundaries do the same; they protect your time, focus, and energy from being stretched too thin or used unfairly. For Black women, setting and upholding boundaries is more than just saying "no" to extra work; it's about claiming your professional space with clarity and respect. Boundaries protect against burnout, preserve your mental and physical health, and ensure that your contributions remain sustainable over the long term.

For example, consider a scenario where a colleague frequently delegates last-minute tasks to you, assuming you'll step in to "help the team." While one or two instances might seem manageable, a pattern like this can lead to blurred lines, with your reliability mistaken for endless availability. Setting boundaries — like requesting advance notice for assignments or clarifying priorities with your manager — helps ensure your value isn't taken for granted while maintaining professional standards.

Setting boundaries isn't about isolation; it's about creating a structure where you can thrive. Without clear boundaries, others may unintentionally (or intentionally) overstep, leading to unmanageable workloads or, worse, being undervalued despite consistent effort. By defining your limits early and communicating them effectively, you control how you're perceived and respected in the workplace.

Rule Insights

Rule 5: Goalpost's gonna keep shifting. Clear boundaries create a foundation, ensuring you aren't constantly adapting to others' changing demands without regard for your well-being.

Rule 6: Shade is inevitable. Setting firm boundaries minimizes opportunities for misinterpretation or exploitation, shielding you from unnecessary conflict or manipulation.

Strategy for Success

Boundaries are about prioritizing what matters, not closing yourself off. Be clear about your workload, availability, and needs so others understand — and respect — your limits.

- ✓ Define your non-negotiables: Identify what you need to feel balanced and effective, whether it's uninterrupted time for deep work, no late-night emails, or time off that's truly off.
- ✓ Communicate clearly and professionally: When asserting boundaries, frame them as ways to

maintain productivity and collaboration, not as obstacles. For example, "I'm happy to assist, but I'll need [X amount of time] to ensure I can deliver quality results."

✓ Stay consistent: Inconsistently enforced boundaries confuse others and undermine your efforts. Stick to what you've established, even if it initially feels uncomfortable.

✓ Anticipate pushback: Not everyone will respect your boundaries immediately but calmly reaffirming them over time helps others adjust.

✓ Seek reinforcement from allies: If someone continuously oversteps, enlist the help of supportive colleagues or supervisors who can advocate for your time and priorities.

By setting clear boundaries and defending them professionally, you reinforce your role as a key player on the board — one whose time and energy are valuable and respected.

Document, Document, Document

Keeping track of moves in chess allows players to study strategy, anticipate threats, and avoid repeating mistakes. In corporate spaces, documentation serves the same purpose — your record of facts, preserving your contributions, decisions, and achievements. For Black women, maintaining a detailed paper trail is more than just a best practice; it's an essential defense. When you document, you protect yourself from misrepresentation, revisionist narratives, or attempts to diminish your role.

Imagine this: You're approaching a performance review, and you hear through the grapevine that your manager has flagged you as "difficult to work with." This vague label feels unfounded, especially since you've delivered results consistently and have received positive feedback from colleagues. Without documentation, countering this claim might feel impossible. But if you've kept a record of positive emails, successful project milestones, and even verbal praise documented in follow-up emails, you're prepared to present a factual narrative. By doing so, you challenge the inaccuracies and ensure the focus remains on your work and not on baseless perceptions.

Documentation is essential in environments where Black women often face heightened scrutiny. It safeguards against biases and helps counteract the invisibility of others misrepresenting or overlooking your contributions. More than that, it builds a career timeline, showing growth, successes, and the challenges you've overcome. Your paper trail isn't just a defense — it's a testament to your journey.

Rule Insights

Rule 5: Goalpost's gonna keep shifting. Documentation ensures that your contributions are clear and undeniable, no matter how expectations or standards change.

Rule 7: Ain't nobody coming to save you. Keeping your own records means you're always prepared to advocate for yourself rather than relying on others to validate your achievements.

Strategy for Success

From day one, make documentation an integral part of your workflow. This habit ensures you're ready to defend your contributions and showcase your value at any moment.

- ✓ Track milestones and achievements: Log every project, deliverable, and measurable result. Regularly update a portfolio or document that outlines your professional impact.
- ✓ Document key conversations: Summarize decisions or next steps via email after important meetings. For example, "Per our conversation, here's what we discussed and agreed upon..." ensures a clear record.
- ✓ Save positive and constructive feedback: Collect emails, performance reviews, or verbal feedback (noted privately afterward) to support your narrative during appraisals or disputes.
- ✓ Maintain a timeline of your progress: Keep a professional journal or spreadsheet that outlines your role in key projects, promotions, and any shifts in responsibilities.

✓ Use documentation to prepare for reviews or disputes: A detailed record gives you the confidence to present your case clearly and factually when preparing for performance reviews or challenging misperceptions.

By documenting consistently, you claim your narrative, ensuring that your contributions remain visible and grounded in facts, no matter the circumstances. It's not just about defense—it's about building and preserving your career's legacy.

Disability Coverage as Your Escape Hatch

In chess, skilled players anticipate potential risks and prepare to adapt. In corporate life, this means having a safety net, like disability coverage, which allows you to prioritize your health without risking financial stability. For Black women, who may face heightened stress in unsupportive environments, disability coverage can be the escape hatch that protects your well-being. Disability coverage provides the space to heal and regroup without the added anxiety of financial instability. It's not just a safeguard—it's a strategic tool to reclaim control when circumstances demand a pause.

Rule Insights

Rule 1: Nobody talks about playing the game. Few openly discuss the importance of disability coverage as part of career strategy. Recognizing its value and incorporating it into your plans positions you ahead of the game, ensuring you're prepared for circumstances that others might overlook.

Rule 5: Goalpost's gonna keep shifting. Corporate priorities and workplace dynamics can change without warning, often increasing stress and pressure. Having disability coverage ensures that you're prepared for these shifts, allowing you to prioritize your health and financial stability when the unexpected happens.

Strategy for Success

Building a safety net through disability coverage requires intentional planning and attention to detail. By understanding your options and aligning them with your financial and career goals, you can ensure that you're protected when life's unexpected challenges arise. These strategies will help you maximize your benefits and maintain stability while prioritizing your health and well-being.

- ✓ Maximize Employer Benefits: If your employer offers disability insurance, make sure you're enrolled in both short- and long-term plans. Review the policy details to understand what percentage of your income will be covered and for how long.
- ✓ Fill the Gaps: If your company's plan doesn't provide full income coverage, consider purchasing a supplementary policy. Look for options that align with your financial needs, covering up to 60-70% of your salary.
- ✓ Understand the Fine Print: Disability coverage can vary widely. Review waiting periods, exclusions, and what constitutes a qualifying event. This knowledge

ensures you're prepared to activate your benefits when needed.

✓ Budget for Premiums: If supplemental insurance requires out-of-pocket costs, factor this into your financial plan. View it as an investment in your long-term security.

✓ Prioritize Health Maintenance: Disability coverage is your escape hatch, but preventive care reduces the likelihood of needing it. Regular checkups and stress management are critical to maintaining overall well-being.

✓ Seek Legal or Financial Advice: If navigating disability benefits feels complex, consult a professional. An HR representative, financial planner, or attorney can help you fully leverage your coverage.

✓ Share Knowledge Strategically: While discussing your coverage at work isn't necessary, sharing insights with trusted colleagues or mentees can create awareness about the importance of this safety net—helping others build their own escape hatches.

Disability coverage is a powerful but often overlooked part of your career strategy. It's not just about preparing for the worst; it's about ensuring you have the resources to prioritize your well-being when the unexpected arises. By integrating disability coverage into your financial and career plans, you create the flexibility to focus on what matters most: your health and future.

Back Pocket Defense: Freelancing and Flexibility

One of the most effective ways to safeguard your career and maintain control is by building a back pocket defense—a source of flexible income or a side hustle that can provide a safety net in uncertain times. For Black women navigating corporate America, having an opportunity in your back pocket ensures you're never fully reliant on a single role or organization for your financial stability.

Whether it's freelancing, consulting, or working a flexible part-time job, this additional income stream creates freedom. It allows you to take a step back from toxic environments, say no to compromising opportunities, or bridge gaps during transitions. Beyond income, it's an opportunity to sharpen your skills, expand your network, and diversify your professional portfolio.

Having this built-in flexibility is more than a financial cushion—it's a way to maintain your power and autonomy in the face of unexpected challenges or shifting priorities in the workplace.

Strategy for Success

Here are actionable steps to create and sustain a back pocket defense:

- ✓ Identify Your Strengths: Choose a side hustle or freelance opportunity that leverages your existing skills or passions. Writing, graphic design, consulting, tutoring, or virtual assistance are great starting points.
- ✓ Start Small: Begin with manageable commitments—weekend gigs, evening work, or small projects

that fit your schedule. Gradually increase your involvement if it aligns with your goals.

✓ Use Freelancing Platforms: Explore platforms like Upwork, Fiverr, or LinkedIn to find opportunities that match your expertise.

✓ Stay Organized: Balance your main role and side hustle by managing your time effectively. Tools like calendars and project management software can help you stay on top of deadlines.

✓ Reinvest in Yourself: Use your side income to build savings, pay down debt, or invest in professional development that strengthens both your primary career and freelance opportunities.

✓ Network Strategically: Freelancing can expand your circle. Stay connected to the clients and contacts you work with—they may open doors to new opportunities.

✓ Reassess Periodically: Regularly evaluate your side hustle's value. Is it still supporting your goals? Does it provide the flexibility you need? Adjust as necessary to keep it aligned with your aspirations.

Rule Insights

Rule 7: Ain't nobody coming to Save you. Your Back Pocket Defense is the ultimate self-reliance strategy. It ensures that, no matter the challenges you face in corporate America, you have options to support yourself and make independent decisions.

Rule 2: There are no spectators. Even your freelance work or side hustle contributes to your career journey. Every connection, skill, and success strengthen your overall trajectory.

Rule 5: Goalpost's gonna keep shifting. A flexible income stream ensures that when corporate demands shift or expectations change, you remain grounded. You're not just reacting to changes — you're proactively securing your future.

From Freelancing to Financial Freedom

The Back Pocket Defense is an immediate, actionable way to create financial security and flexibility, but it's only one part of the broader picture. Financial

Resilience, the next step, builds on this foundation to ensure your long-term stability and freedom to navigate your career on your terms.

Financial Freedom

Just as the Rook provides structure on the chessboard, financial security offers stability in your career. A solid financial foundation allows you to choose from a place of empowerment rather than necessity. For Black women, financial independence isn't just about security; it's a form of freedom that lets you walk away from toxic situations and pursue new opportunities on your terms.

Strategy for Success

Build a savings cushion and manage expenses carefully. Financial resilience secures you and gives you the freedom to make value-based choices.

Rule Insights

Rule 7: Ain't Nobody Coming to Save You. In corporate America, your financial well-being is your responsibility. A strong foundation allows you to make choices that protect your interests and to walk away when necessary.

Knowing Your Rights

When playing the game of corporate America, few pieces are more vital than understanding your legal rights. The Equal Employment Opportunity Commission (EEOC) enforces laws protecting employees from workplace discrimination. Yet, many Black women remain unaware of how these protections apply to them — or of the strict timelines that govern filing a charge of discrimination. Knowing your rights isn't just an abstract principle; it's a critical defense mechanism, particularly in workplaces where bias, microaggressions, and outright discrimination often go unchecked.

One of the most critical pieces of information to understand is that the clock starts ticking the moment discrimination occurs. Whether it's a demotion, termination, pay disparity, harassment, or other discriminatory action, your window to act is limited. In most cases, employees have 180 days from the incident date to file a charge with the EEOC. However, if your state has a fair employment practices agency with additional protections, the window can extend to 300 days. This variance makes it crucial to know your state's specific guidelines. Miss that window, and no matter how airtight your case or how comprehensive your documentation is, your claim likely won't move forward.

This time limitation underscores why documentation and awareness of your rights are essential parts of your professional defense system. Many Black women endure workplace discrimination without taking immediate action, whether out of fear of retaliation, uncertainty about the process, or a desire to avoid confrontation. But in doing so, they unknowingly forfeit one of their most powerful forms of recourse. Taking proactive steps, seeking legal counsel, consulting your HR department, or contacting the EEOC directly, you're prepared to act if needed.

Key Steps to Protect Yourself

1. Know the timeline for your state. Familiarize yourself with both federal and state-level guidelines

for filing discrimination charges. Research into whether your state offers an extended filing period beyond the EEOC's standard 180 days.

2. Document the incident thoroughly. Immediately after experiencing discrimination, write down a detailed account of what happened. Include dates, times, individuals involved, and any witnesses. Supporting evidence like emails, texts, or meeting records strengthens your case.

3. Consult with HR—but cautiously. While HR can be a resource, their primary role is to protect the company. Approach any discussions carefully, keeping detailed notes of all interactions, and consider involving an attorney if the situation escalates.

4. File sooner rather than later. The earlier you file a charge, the more credibility your case holds. Waiting too long may weaken your claim, even if it falls within the deadline.

5. Seek legal counsel. If you need clarification on your rights or the process, consult an employment lawyer familiar with workplace discrimination cases. Many offer free consultations to assess the strength of your claim.

Filing an EEOC Claim While Still Employed

It's a common misconception that you must leave your employer before filing a discrimination charge with the EEOC. In reality, staying employed while filing a claim can be one of your most strategic moves. Filing while still employed provides the additional protection of anti-retaliation laws, which prohibit your employer from taking adverse actions against you for exercising your rights. This means they cannot legally demote you, reduce your pay, terminate your employment, or create a hostile work environment in response to your claim. Understanding this protection can embolden you to act without fear of immediate repercussions.

Filing as a current employee can also serve a practical purpose. Often, discrimination claims stem from ongoing behaviors or decisions, such as being repeatedly passed over for promotions, unequal pay, or unfair performance evaluations. Addressing these issues while they're still happening strengthens your case and ensures you remain within the filing window. Waiting until you've left the organization could put you outside that critical timeframe, leaving you without legal recourse. Filing early sends a clear message that you know your rights and are willing to stand up for them.

Furthermore, filing a claim while employed can sometimes spark positive organizational change. Although it's not guaranteed, many companies use the EEOC process as an opportunity to review internal practices, mediate issues, and, in some cases, resolve claims before they escalate. Regardless of the outcome, taking action early allows you to reclaim your power and advocate for yourself without letting fear of retaliation or misunderstanding of your rights keep you silent.

Rule Insights

Rule 7: Ain't nobody coming to save you. Understanding and leveraging the protections available to you ensure you're not waiting for an external ally to intervene. Your rights are your armor, but it's up to you to use them.

Rule 2: There are no spectators. Just as you can't afford to be passive in the game, you can't delay action when discrimination arises. Timely responses are how you defend your position on the board.

Strategy for Success

Protecting yourself in the workplace isn't just about being prepared, it's about taking intentional steps to safeguard your career, reputation, and well-being. The strategies below provide a roadmap for ensuring that, even in challenging environments, you remain prepared and in control of your path forward.

- ✓ Educate yourself on your rights. Familiarize yourself with federal and state protections to ensure you're equipped to act if discrimination arises.

✓ Keep a record of discriminatory incidents. Detailed documentation strengthens your position and makes your case more challenging to dismiss.

✓ Stay vigilant about timelines. Be mindful of the EEOC's filing deadlines to avoid losing your opportunity for recourse.

✓ Act proactively, not reactively. Whether you consult an attorney or contact the EEOC, moving quickly after an incident protects your options.

Knowing your EEOC protections is a critical part of playing the game. When discrimination arises, your ability to act decisively can mean the difference between finding justice or being sidelined. Don't wait until it's too late. Arm yourself with knowledge and the tools to protect your career.

Prioritize Your Emotional Well-being

In chess, the queen's power hinges on her position and the protection the pieces around her provide. In corporate spaces, emotional well-being serves as your foundation, enabling you to withstand the pressures and demands of the game. For Black women, prioritizing mental health isn't just an option—it's a necessity. Guarding your crown means safeguarding the core of who you are, ensuring that you remain strong, balanced, and unshaken despite the challenges that may come your way.

The workplace can be rife with pressures—microaggressions, heightened expectations, and systemic barriers—that weigh heavily on your emotional health. It's easy to fall into the trap of trying to prove your worth through relentless overperformance, neglecting your mental well-being. But protecting your crown requires reframing what strength looks like. Strength isn't just about endurance; it's about knowing when to pause, recharge, and set boundaries that preserve your peace.

Picture this: you're tasked with leading a high-visibility project alongside your regular workload. The pressure to perform flawlessly, particularly as a Black woman, feels overwhelming. Rather than shouldering it silently, you advocate for yourself, communicating your capacity and requesting additional resources to support the project. By doing so, you deliver excellent work and demonstrate that your boundaries and mental health are priorities. This act of self-advocacy protects your emotional balance while reinforcing your professional credibility.

Rule Insights

Rule 3: Their best is your mediocre. Prioritizing emotional well-being ensures you're equipped to meet high expectations without compromising your inner balance or allowing yourself to be consumed by the pressure.

Rule 5: Goalpost's gonna keep shifting. Protecting your emotional well-being is vital in workplaces where expectations are constantly changing. It helps you remain adaptable and grounded, even as the game's rules evolve around you.

Strategy for Success

Your emotional well-being is the cornerstone of your strength, shaping how you navigate challenges and maintain resilience in demanding corporate environments. Protecting your crown begins with recognizing that self-care isn't selfish, it's essential. By prioritizing your mental health, you set the tone for how others respect your boundaries and value your contributions.

- ✓ Recognize stress signals early: Pay attention to physical, mental, and emotional signs of burnout. Address them proactively by implementing regular self-check-ins.
- ✓ Invest in your mental health: Therapy, mindfulness practices, and even small daily rituals like journaling or meditation can create a buffer against workplace stress.
- ✓ Set boundaries unapologetically: Learn to say no or delegate when demands exceed your capacity. Protecting your peace is a strength, not a weakness.

✓ Advocate for yourself: Don't be afraid to communicate your needs or limitations in a professional and solution-oriented way. When necessary, advocate for additional support or resources.

✓ Build a support network: Surround yourself with mentors, allies, and trusted colleagues who can offer perspective, validation, and encouragement when work feels overwhelming.

Guarding your crown means understanding that mental health is critical to your success. Protecting your well-being ensures that your foundation remains strong, allowing you to navigate challenges and claim your space with resilience and purpose.

Build a Supportive Network

Just as a knight in chess provides defense by covering various positions, a strong network is your shield, offering support and guidance when challenges arise. For Black women navigating corporate spaces, allies, mentors, and advocates provide critical layers of defense, helping to counter biases, amplify achievements, and protect against isolation. A well-rounded network isn't just beneficial, it's essential for building resilience and ensuring your professional growth.

By cultivating authentic connections, you gain access to diverse perspectives, insights into workplace dynamics, and advocates who can champion your work when you're not in the room. Your network becomes a fortress, ensuring you're well-positioned to navigate the complexities of your career while staying grounded in your goals.

Rule Insights

Rule 4: There can only be one. Building allies ensures you're not navigating alone in environments that often pit us against one another. A strong network reinforces the idea that collaboration, not competition, drives success, even in restrictive spaces.

Rule 7: Ain't nobody coming to save you. In corporate spaces where stability and advocacy aren't guaranteed, proactively building your network ensures you have the support you need to thrive. Allies and mentors become your first line of defense, giving you a stronger foothold.

Strategy for Success:

Building a supportive network starts with intention. Your network should be more than just a collection of contacts, your safety net, source of perspective, and launchpad for growth. Establishing authentic relationships with allies, mentors, and advocates ensures you're not navigating the complexities of corporate spaces alone. These connections provide strategic guidance and emotional reinforcement, helping you weather challenges and confidently seize opportunities.

- ✓ Identify potential allies: Look for individuals across departments or levels who have influence, share your values, or are willing to mentor you. Diversify your network to include colleagues with varied expertise and perspectives.
- ✓ Be intentional about outreach: Building a network requires effort. Make time to connect with others through

regular check-ins, collaborative projects, or informal conversations.

✓ Show appreciation: Acknowledge the contributions and support of your allies. Gratitude fosters stronger relationships and ensures your connections remain genuine.

✓ Offer reciprocal support: Relationships thrive when both parties benefit. Be willing to advocate for others, share resources, and celebrate their successes.

✓ Leverage your network strategically: When facing challenges or pursuing new opportunities, tap into your network for advice, advocacy, and introductions. Allies can open doors and amplify your voice.

A strong network is one of the most valuable assets in your career. It reinforces your position, protects against isolation, and allows you to navigate with greater confidence. By cultivating authentic and mutually beneficial relationships, you create a community of support that grows with you, ensuring your success isn't just sustainable but shared.

Above Reproach: Maintain Integrity

A strong reputation is like a castle: once fortified, it's difficult to dismantle. Integrity provides a defense that speaks for itself, reinforcing trust, commanding respect, and allowing you to navigate even the most challenging environments authentically. But integrity isn't always easy, nor is it without cost.

Integrity has been the cornerstone of everything I do, often to my detriment. Let's consider a scenario that might sound familiar: You're part of a high-visibility team project, and during a critical review, a colleague "embellishes" the results to make the outcomes appear more favorable. The temptation to let it slide can be tempting—after all, you don't want to be seen as a disruptor or jeopardize the team's success. But instead, you decide to speak up, gently correcting the narrative and offering an honest, clear assessment of the project's status. Your decision keeps the team accountable, but not everyone appreciates it. Whispers start circulating that you're too rigid or overly critical, casting doubt on your ability to be a "team player." The fallout feels isolating at first, but in the right environment, your integrity and consistency build trust with leadership over time, while the team's eventual success reinforces your value.

For Black women, the stakes of maintaining integrity are even higher. It's not just about doing what's right, it's about proving that our success is earned, not given. It's about countering stereotypes and ensuring that we leave no room for doubt about the value we bring.

However, integrity can be a double-edged sword, especially when bending the truth or shading details is treated as standard operating procedure. Toxic workplaces often create unspoken norms that reward results at any cost — even if it means sacrificing transparency or ethics. In these spaces, sticking to your principles can make you stand out for the wrong reasons. You might find yourself labeled as "difficult," "too rigid," or "not a team player" simply because you refuse to play along with the office culture of dishonesty. The pressure to conform, to fudge the numbers, or to stay silent in the face of questionable practices can feel overwhelming.

A critical decision must be made: What is more important to you? Is it maintaining your integrity, even if it means facing pushback, isolation, or slower career progression? Or is it staying in lockstep with the environment, even at the expense of your values? Neither choice is easy, and you alone can determine the right or wrong choice for you. Ultimately, it depends on your goals, your boundaries, and the toll you're willing to endure. What's crucial is understanding that this decision is yours to make, and no one else can dictate what matters most to you. Choosing integrity may come at a cost, but it also ensures that you can stand firm in who you are, even when the culture around you feels shaky.

In some cases, maintaining your integrity will mean staying and fighting the good fight, finding allies who share your values, and setting a higher standard. In others, it may mean recognizing that the environment isn't worthy of your efforts and deciding to leave. Knowing what matters most to you will help you navigate these challenges with clarity and conviction.

Strategy for Success

Maintaining integrity in the workplace is both a shield and a challenge. It provides a solid foundation for trust and long-term success, but it often requires courage to uphold, especially in environments where dishonesty or ethical shortcuts are normalized. To navigate this effectively, you need a strategy that balances your principles with the realities of the workplace.

- ✓ Set your non-negotiables: Identify the values you won't compromise on, regardless of the situation. Knowing your boundaries beforehand ensures you can make clear decisions under pressure.
- ✓ Document everything: Integrity doesn't just rely on honesty — it also relies on accountability. Keep a detailed record of your contributions, decisions, and

conversations to reinforce your credibility if challenged.

✓ Gauge the environment: Take stock of your workplace culture. Is it one where integrity is valued or one where questionable practices are tolerated? Understanding the dynamics can help you decide whether to stay and fight for change or explore opportunities elsewhere.

✓ Build a support system: Align with colleagues, mentors, or leaders who share your values. When your integrity is tested, these allies can provide perspective, advocacy, and encouragement.

✓ Practice discretion: While it's important to speak up for what's right, choosing when and how to raise concerns is equally critical. Frame your points as constructive rather than critical to minimize backlash in hostile environments.

✓ Evaluate your decisions regularly: Revisit how your commitment to integrity aligns with your long-term goals. If upholding your

principles threatens your well-being or career trajectory, it may be
time to reassess your options.

Choosing integrity is rarely easy, but it sets you apart as a reliable, trustworthy professional. While the cost of sticking to your principles can sometimes feel isolating, over time, it builds a reputation that no one can dismantle. When you protect your integrity, you're not just playing the game but elevating the board itself.

An Ironclad Defense for Long-Term Success

Building a defense in corporate America isn't about staying stagnant; it's about fortifying your position, preserving your values, and preparing for whatever the future holds. By cultivating financial, legal, emotional, and strategic defenses, you create a protective foundation that empowers you to navigate corporate spaces confidently, regardless of obstacles.

Key Takeaways

- ❖ Establish Clear Boundaries: Like a pawn wall in chess, boundaries protect your time, energy, and focus. Define and communicate them clearly to maintain your professional space.
- ❖ Document Everything: Keeping detailed records of your contributions, achievements, and key conversations safeguards your narrative and protects your credibility in the workplace.
- ❖ Build Financial Resilience: A strong financial foundation gives you the freedom to make empowered decisions and leave toxic environments if necessary.
- ❖ Prioritize Your Well-being: Protecting your mental health is as critical as guarding your professional reputation. Regular self-care ensures you're equipped to handle challenges without burnout.
- ❖ Understand Disability Coverage: Investigate your workplace benefits and consider external

supplemental disability insurance to ensure financial stability if health challenges arise.

❖ Cultivate a Support Network: Build strong alliances across departments and roles to reinforce your defenses and create support opportunities when needed.

❖ Seek Legal Counsel Strategically: Establish connections with a legal advisor early in your career to understand your rights and seek objective guidance when workplace challenges escalate.

❖ Adaptability Is Power: Embrace flexibility in your career to navigate shifting goalposts and changes in corporate priorities. Your ability to pivot is a cornerstone of resilience.

❖ Maintain Integrity: A reputation built on honesty and ethical conduct acts as your ultimate defense, speaking volumes when adversity strikes.

Food for Thought

- ❖ **Reflect:** Are your current boundaries protecting your time and mental health? Identify one area where you need to strengthen them and take a small step this week to reinforce that boundary.
- ❖ **Challenge:** Start documenting your professional achievements and interactions today. Whether it's an email folder, a notebook, or a digital file. Create a habit of keeping track of your contributions and key workplace events.

Chapter 10: Check, Not Mate

In chess, calling "check" can shift the entire game's dynamic, but it doesn't finish it. It's a move of foresight and precision, designed to press pause and force the opponent to consider their next steps carefully. In the corporate world, this "Check, Not Mate" idea resonates deeply, especially for Black women. Strategic restraint—knowing when to pause, when to pull back, and when to hold your ground—is an art that lets you advance without stepping into every battle. This chapter is about wielding that power of patience and discernment, understanding that moving forward isn't always about charging ahead; sometimes, it's about staying rooted in place and watching the board.

Knowing When to Hold 'Em

The temptation to push forward at every opportunity can be overwhelming in the corporate arena. The pressure to prove yourself, to be visible, and to tackle every challenge head-on often feels like a mandate—especially for Black women who are constantly fighting against stereotypes and underestimation. But the truth is, relentless action without a strategy can leave you overexposed and vulnerable. Just as a seasoned chess player knows when to hold off on a move to avoid jeopardizing their position, knowing when to step back is critical in the corporate game.

Stepping back isn't about weakness or complacency; it's a calculated act of restraint. Restraint allows you to observe the board, weigh your options, and conserve energy for the battles that matter most. Discerning which fights are worth your time is an underrated form of power in an environment where shade is inevitable. It's about realizing that not every challenge, slight, or setback demands an immediate response. Sometimes, the strongest move is no move at all.

Consider this: You're in a meeting, and a colleague throws a thinly veiled jab at your performance. The room shifts uncomfortably, all eyes darting between you and the speaker. You could respond immediately, defending yourself and addressing the insult head-on. But what if doing so plays into the narrative they're trying to create — that you're overly sensitive or combative? Instead, you let the comment hang in the air, its pettiness speaking for itself. Later, you strategically address the situation with the decision-maker who matters, framing your response to reinforce your professionalism and focus. That moment of restraint keeps your energy intact while shifting the power dynamic in your favor.

Rule Insights

Rule 6: Shade is Inevitable. In corporate spaces, shade often comes in subtle, insidious forms designed to provoke a reaction. But not every jab deserves a counter. Practicing restraint lets you sidestep unnecessary drama, conserve energy, and refocus on the battles that truly matter. Restraint is the quiet power that reminds others you are in control, unshaken by their attempts to derail you.

Strategy for Success

Restraint is a skill that requires intentional practice. Learning to pause and reflect before acting strengthens your ability to navigate complex situations with clarity and purpose. Here are strategies to help you hone this critical skill:

- ✓ Ask yourself, "Will this serve my long-term vision?" Before reacting to any situation, take a moment to assess whether engaging will help or hinder your broader goals. If the answer is unclear, step back and give yourself time to gain perspective.
- ✓ Master the art of observation. Use moments of restraint to watch, listen, and gather information. Often, staying quiet allows you to uncover dynamics or patterns you might have missed if you had acted impulsively.
- ✓ Prioritize your energy. Focus on the challenges that truly matter to your career trajectory. Let go of the smaller battles that only serve to distract you from your larger goals.

✓ Choose your timing wisely. Restraint doesn't mean avoiding confrontation altogether—it means addressing issues when you are fully prepared, and the timing works to your advantage.

✓ Practice emotional detachment. Not every slight or challenge is a reflection of your value. By separating your emotions from your strategy, you're better equipped to respond with poise and intention.

Knowing when to step back is an act of self-preservation, recognizing that your energy is finite, and your goals are worth protecting. It's not about surrender or avoidance—it's about playing the long game with precision and grace. By mastering the art of restraint, you position yourself as a strategic thinker who moves with intention and clarity. You're not just surviving the board but reshaping it in your favor, one deliberate move at a time.

The Strategic Retreat

A well-timed retreat in chess provides space to reassess and watch how the board shifts. In corporate life, stepping back isn't about defeat but letting others reveal their intentions. For Black women navigating the complexities of workplace dynamics, a strategic retreat allows for recalibration without the pressure to respond immediately. It's a moment to pause, observe, and consider your next move with intention.

The power of retreat lies in its ability to shift the focus away from you, allowing you to analyze the dynamics at play. Sometimes, letting others take the lead exposes motives, patterns, or weaknesses you wouldn't have noticed in the moment. This isn't passivity, it's the art of waiting for the right moment to engage, equipped with insight and clarity.

Rule Insights

Rule 5: *Goalpost's gonna keep shifting.* Corporate environments often demand constant adjustment, with priorities and expectations shifting without warning. Taking a strategic step back allows you to watch how the board evolves, ensuring you're not reacting impulsively to changes. When you reengage, you'll do so from a place of strength and clarity, prepared to meet the shifting demands head-on.

Strategy for Success

Before engaging in a situation, consider whether stepping back would offer a better vantage point. A strategic retreat uses pauses to your advantage, allowing you to assess and prepare for the right moment to act. Here's how to make it work:

- ✓ Ask yourself, "Is my involvement truly necessary?" Assess whether engaging in a situation adds value or drains your energy. If the answer is no, step back and let others move first.
- ✓ Use pauses to observe. A retreat isn't idle—it's a moment to analyze the board. Watch how others respond or take control, gaining insights about your next move.
- ✓ Don't feel pressured to fill the silence. Letting others fill the void often reveals their priorities,

motivations, or weaknesses. Use this information to guide your strategy.

✓ Preserve your energy for high-stakes moves. A strategic retreat ensures you're not wasting effort on minor battles, keeping you focused on the challenges that truly matter.

✓ Be deliberate when you reengage. When you decide to act, do so with intention and clarity, ensuring your move aligns with your long-term goals.

A strategic retreat isn't a sign of weakness, it's a demonstration of foresight. By stepping back, you create space to recalibrate, analyze, and prepare for the next move. It's about choosing action over reaction, ensuring that you're equipped with the insight and confidence to make a lasting impact when you reengage. The power of retreat lies in knowing when to pause and when to strike, always keeping your long-term vision in sight.

The Art of Holding Space

In chess, taking a moment to study the board allows players to anticipate moves with greater insight. In the workplace, holding space functions in the same way. Instead of rushing to respond, silence and observation often reveal the intentions and underlying dynamics. For Black women, who frequently face environments of heightened scrutiny, using silence as a tool to assess can be transformative. It's not about disengaging—it's about creating room to think critically and strategically. Silence isn't inaction; it's a deliberate choice to pause, reflect, and assess your next move with precision.

Holding space provides a moment to refocus and recalibrate. While others might quickly fill the silence with assumptions or assertions, your stillness becomes an opportunity to observe power structures, alliances, and hidden agendas. Choosing not to rush into action allows you to see the broader picture, setting the stage for thoughtful, impactful engagement.

Imagine you're in a meeting discussing the next steps for a high-profile project. Tensions are high, and people are vying to showcase their ideas, speaking over each other to gain the manager's approval. As the conversation intensifies, you notice some questionable suggestions being accepted without scrutiny. Instead of jumping into the fray, you choose to hold space, listening intently while mentally noting fundamental dynamics — who supports whom, who speaks without interruption, and whose ideas are dismissed outright.

Later, during a one-on-one with your manager, you bring up your observations. You share your concerns about certain decisions' overlooked implications while positioning your ideas as solutions. Your silence during the meeting wasn't passive; it allowed you to gather insights and strategically address them in a way that commanded respect and attention.

Rule Insights

Rule 7: Ain't nobody coming to save you. Holding space allows you to see who's genuinely on your side, who remains neutral, and who may pose challenges. By leaning into observation, you build self-reliance, positioning yourself to navigate with clarity and intentionality. In environments where trust can be scarce, holding space strengthens your ability to steer your own course confidently.

Strategy for Success

Silence and stillness are underrated tools in corporate spaces. Use them to create room for intentional action. Here's how to make holding space an effective strategy:

- ✓ Recognize the power of silence. Instead of rushing to respond, take a moment to pause and observe. Silence can disarm others and create space for deeper understanding.
- ✓ Study dynamics carefully. Watch how people interact and align. Look for patterns in their behavior and relationships that might signal where power truly lies.
- ✓ Choose engagement deliberately. Hold space to determine whether

your involvement will add value. When you decide to act, ensure it's with intention and purpose.

✓ Use pauses to clarify your perspective. Holding space allows you to process emotions and avoid knee-jerk reactions, ensuring that your response aligns with your values and goals.

✓ Signal strength through your stillness. Silence can command as much respect as words when deliberate, signaling that you're present, observant, and intentional.

Holding space isn't about stepping back, it's about stepping forward with focus and clarity. By creating moments of stillness, you center yourself in environments that often demand immediate reactions. The ability to pause, observe, and act purposefully reinforces your influence, ensuring that every move you make is meaningful and impactful.

Pick Your Battles Wisely

Not every fight in the workplace is worth waging. Embracing the "Check, Not Mate" mindset is about prioritizing conflicts that align with your goals and letting go of distractions. By reserving your energy for battles that truly count, you protect your focus and strengthen your ability to advance strategically. Restraint is not avoidance or weakness; it's intentional prioritization. Choosing your battles wisely ensures you remain effective and impactful without exhausting yourself over unnecessary distractions.

For Black women in corporate spaces, the stakes of every disagreement can feel heightened, with each conflict potentially being framed as "too much" or "too aggressive." This makes discerning which battles to fight all the more critical. It's about understanding when to push forward and when to step back, always ensuring that your efforts align with your larger vision.

Imagine a colleague interrupts you repeatedly during meetings, subtly undermining your points. It's frustrating, but you recognize that directly confronting this behavior might escalate into a conflict that could distract from your current focus: securing a leadership position.

Instead, you choose a strategic approach. You address the behavior indirectly by ensuring your contributions are documented and shared with the team after the meeting. You also schedule a one-on-one with your manager to highlight your key insights, making it clear that your voice is critical to the team's success.

Rather than engaging in an immediate confrontation, you prioritize the larger goal of demonstrating your leadership skills. Over time, your manager's acknowledgment of your impact shifts the dynamics, while your restraint ensures you don't waste energy on a conflict that might derail your trajectory.

Rule Insights

Rule 6: Shade is inevitable. Not every slight or challenge requires a response. Recognizing when shade is just, noise allows you to conserve your energy for the moments that truly matter. This focus ensures you're advancing where it counts rather than getting caught up in distractions.

Strategy for Success

Fighting every battle can be draining and counterproductive. Focus on those conflicts that align with your goals and position you for success:

- ✓ Assess the stakes. Before engaging in a conflict, ask yourself, "Will this matter six months from now?" Prioritize issues that have long-term significance over short-term frustrations.
- ✓ Align with your goals. If the conflict doesn't directly support your larger vision, consider whether it's worth pursuing. Save your energy for fights that contribute to your growth or credibility.
- ✓ Engage strategically. Address issues in ways that demonstrate leadership and composure. Document your contributions, involve allies, and focus on solutions rather than escalating tensions.
- ✓ Avoid reactive responses. Pause before reacting to slights or provocations. This gives you time to decide whether a response is

necessary or if silence will serve you better.
- ✓ Use restraint to your advantage. Choosing not to engage in every conflict signals strength and focus, showing that you're above unnecessary drama.

Picking your battles isn't about surrendering, it's about playing the long game. Focusing on the conflicts that align with your goals and values allows you to succeed without losing sight of what truly matters. Restraint isn't passivity; it's strategy, ensuring that every move you make is deliberate, impactful, and aligned with your vision for success.

Resilience Through Balance

The heart of "Check, Not Mate" is balancing action with restraint. In chess, advancing recklessly can expose your pieces, but a calculated approach builds strength and ensures longevity. This balance becomes even more critical for Black women navigating the unique workplace challenges. Striking the right balance between engagement and strategic pauses helps reinforce resilience, allowing you to weather setbacks and stay on track toward your goals. True resilience isn't just about enduring pressure, it's about choosing when to act or step back, ensuring that your efforts align with the bigger picture.

For example, you may be asked to take on additional responsibilities that don't align with your long-term goals. The temptation might be to say yes to avoid being perceived as uncooperative. However, exercising restraint by diplomatically declining can protect your focus and ensure your energy is spent on tasks that truly matter. This isn't about saying no for the sake of it; it's about preserving your ability to thrive while staying true to your purpose.

Balance is resilience. It's the ability to combine deliberate action with the wisdom of knowing when to pause. This duality keeps you grounded, adaptable, and prepared to face challenges without compromising your core strengths or values.

Rule Insights

Rule 1: Nobody talks about playing the game. Mastering the balance between visibility and restraint is a critical skill. Knowing when to engage and when to observe shows that success often comes from thoughtful decision-making rather than impulsive actions. This strategic approach becomes a game-changer in corporate America, helping you navigate spaces with clarity and confidence.

Strategy for Success

Building resilience through balance requires thoughtful action and intentional restraint. By evaluating your responses and aligning them with your goals, you create a foundation for long-term success:

- ✓ Evaluate before acting. Pause to consider whether a situation warrants your engagement. Ask yourself, "Does this align with my long-term goals?" before diving in.
- ✓ Preserve your energy. Avoid overcommitting to tasks or conflicts that don't serve your

priorities. Focus on opportunities that enhance your growth and visibility.

✓ Practice mindful restraint. Recognize that not every situation requires an immediate response. Strategic pauses allow you to gain perspective and act with greater clarity.

✓ Stay adaptable. Balance isn't rigid. Be prepared to shift between action and observation as circumstances evolve, ensuring you remain effective and aligned with your vision.

✓ Foster self-reflection. Regularly reassess your strategies and decisions to ensure they align with your values and goals.

Resilience isn't just about enduring—it's about thriving. By mastering the art of balance, you create a powerful framework for navigating challenges while staying true to your goals. The ability to weigh your actions and responses thoughtfully ensures that your every move reinforces your strength, integrity, and long-term success.

The Balance of Action and Restraint

"Check, Not Mate" is the balance strategy—knowing that every situation doesn't demand action. In your career, moving forward doesn't mean taking every opportunity that crosses your path; sometimes, the best moves are the ones you choose not to make. By embracing the "Check, Not Mate" mindset, you create a framework of patience, resilience, and discernment.

Taking strategic pauses, picking battles, and observing sets you up as a powerful presence in any environment. In corporate America, sometimes your strength lies not in charging ahead but in calculated restraint—the wisdom to wait, the courage to hold back, and the insight to respond only when the timing aligns with your vision. You're here for the long game, steady in your path, and prepared to navigate each move with the confidence of a true strategist.

Key Takeaways

- ❖ Know When to Act and When to Pause: Strategic restraint is a tool for advancing with intention, not rushing every opportunity.
- ❖ Pick Your Battles Wisely: Channel your energy toward conflicts that align with your goals and reinforce your long-term vision.
- ❖ Strength in Observation: Observation isn't hesitation; it's the foundation of informed, impactful moves.

Food for Thought

- ❖ **Reflect:** Are there situations in your professional life where acting immediately feels necessary but may not be strategic? What would stepping back reveal?
- ❖ **Challenge:** In your next difficult work encounter, practice holding space. Observe the dynamics without reacting and reflect on the insights you gain.

Nicole S. Palmer

Final Moves: Gratitude, Reflections, and Next Steps

To every Black woman who picked up this book, who saw themselves in these pages, and who trusted me to walk alongside them through this journey: thank you. Writing this book was an act of love and reflection, but it is you who brings its purpose to life. Every moment you spent reading, thinking, and strategizing means the world to me. You've shared a part of your story by simply opening this book, and I hope that in return, you've found insights, strength, and affirmation for your journey.

This book is a culmination of experiences, lessons, and truths that were hard-won. It's my hope that you now feel a little more equipped, a little more empowered, and a lot more confident about navigating the challenges that come your way. Corporate America is no simple terrain, especially for Black women. The game is layered with unspoken rules and shifting dynamics, but it's a game we can win—not by changing who we are but by embracing our brilliance and playing it on our terms.

As I reflect on the chapters we've just traveled through, I want to reiterate this: your journey matters. Every move you make, every step you take forward, is an act of resistance, growth, and power. Whether it's advocating for yourself in a meeting, protecting your crown in the face of bias, or building financial resilience, every action you take shapes the game in your favor.

But this journey isn't just about survival, it's about thriving. It's about creating spaces for yourself and others, challenging the status quo, and showing up with authenticity and pride. It's about understanding that the board is vast, and the pieces are complex, but you, my dear, are the master strategist.

Now that we've walked through these strategies together, I have a challenge for you: don't keep it to yourself. Share what you've learned. Pay it forward to a mentee, a colleague, or someone just stepping onto the board. Build a network that's strong and supportive, because when we lift each other, the game becomes a little less daunting and a lot more winnable.

And if this book has left an impact on you, I'd be incredibly grateful and honored if you would share your honest thoughts in a review. Your voice is powerful, and your perspective could be the one that inspires someone else to pick up this book and start their own journey. Reviews not only help amplify the message but also create a community of readers who are walking this path together.

Your feedback and input are invaluable to me. This book is not static, part of an ongoing conversation about how we navigate and master the game of corporate America. With the paperback edition coming out this summer, I hope to incorporate your thoughts and suggestions to refine this work even further, ensuring it continues to resonate with and serve you. Your voice will shape the next iteration of this book, making it even better for every woman who turns its pages.

As we part ways, I want to leave you with this: You are powerful beyond measure. You are resilient in ways the world has yet to fully recognize. You are strategic, capable, and deserving of every opportunity you claim for yourself. The board may not always be set in your favor, but your moves, your wisdom, and your determination can shift it in ways that matter most.

So, keep playing. Keep thriving. Keep protecting your crown, making bold moves, and embracing your worth. The game is yours to master, and your story is yours to write.

With gratitude and unwavering belief in your brilliance,

Nicole S. Palmer

Nicole S. Palmer

Coming November 2025!

Winning the Game While Black Womaning in Corporate America™ by Nicole S. Palmer

You've read the rules, participants, and opponents. You've made moves with strategy, discernment, and power. Now it's time to win.

Winning the Game is the second install-ment in this bold, unflinching series. It's for every Black woman who's not just navigating the board, but outmaneuver-ing it, despite the traps, shade, despite the system that wasn't built to hold her success.

From subtle power plays to high-stakes wins, this book is your guide to claiming victory on your terms.

Because winning isn't the absence of ad-versity. It's knowing how to move any-way.